Making friends with Money

How to start feeling wealthy
without waiting till you're rich

Sanni Kruger

Making friends with Money

How to start feeling wealthy without waiting till you're rich

Edited by Chris Newton

MEMOIRS

Cirencester

Published by Memoirs

MEMOIRS
P U B L I S H I N G

25 Market Place, Cirencester, Gloucestershire, GL7 2NX
info@memoirsbooks.co.uk www.memoirspublishing.com

Copyright ©Sanni Kruger, September 2011
First published in England, September 2011
Book jacket design Ray Lipscombe

ISBN 978-1-908223-24-1

Printed in England

MAKING FRIENDS WITH MONEY

How to start feeling wealthy without waiting till you're rich

CONTENTS

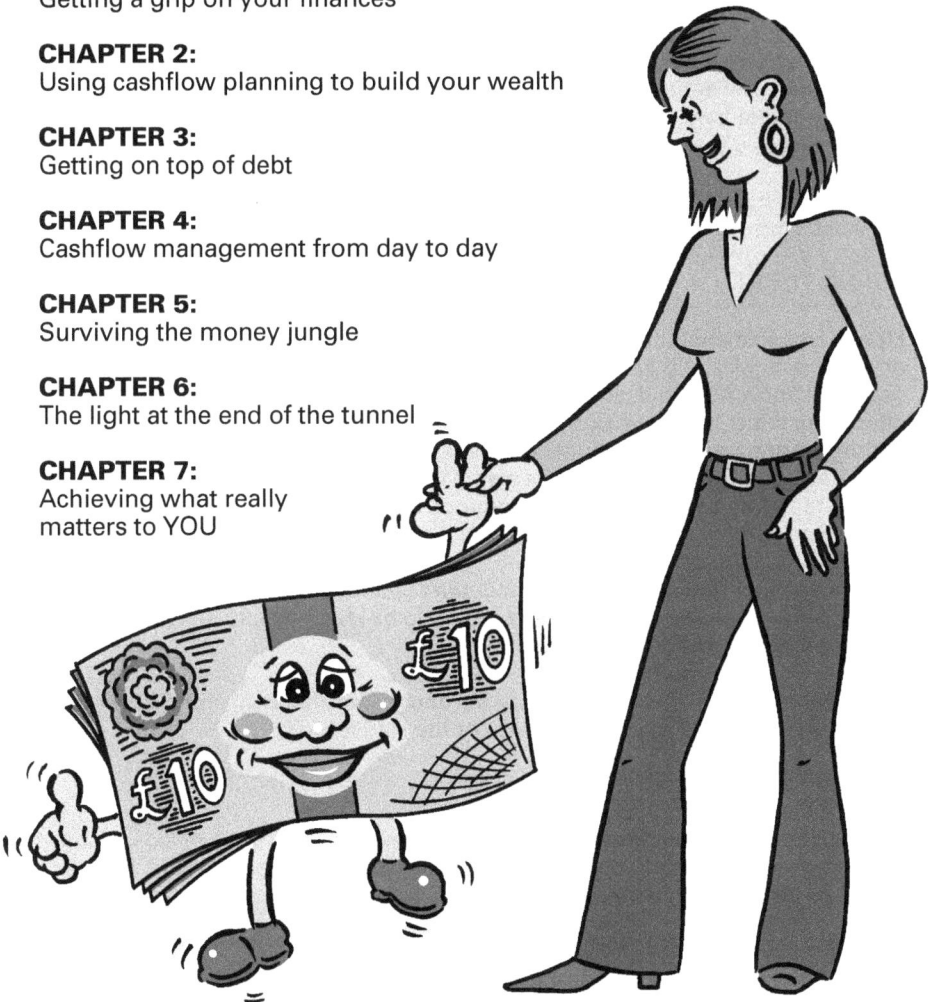

INTRODUCTION

Feeling better about money

Welcome to the definitive step-by-step "How To" guide to:

+ **Managing your money better**
+ **Getting rid of debt**
+ **Building up savings for emergencies, holidays and costly events like Christmas**
+ **Achieving a sense of personal wealth and prosperity**
+ **Identifying your real needs and desires, and the role money should be playing**
+ **Defining and realising your vision**
+ **Discovering a purpose in life, and living it**

This programme is not a quick-fix, get-rich-quick solution. Neither is it about tightening belts and wearing hair shirts. It is much more about changing your **relationship** with the money in your life – however much or little you think you have – so that it helps you to live the way you want, instead of getting in the way.

Following the programme *will* take time, dedication and perseverance – but if you make the commitment to do so, your financial situation will improve.

What **really** matters about money

Money isn't just about the numbers that appear on your monthly bank statement, or how many bills and final demands you keep tucked away in a drawer because you don't know how to deal with them. How much money we have or don't have affects our most basic feelings of safety, security and self-esteem. Money problems can bring unexpected emotional issues to the surface – feelings of insecurity or inadequacy. Some you might be aware of – others you may not. Many people have a terror of being penniless. Some of us are actually afraid of having too much.

Addressing your financial situation shouldn't just be about helping you to afford longer holidays or save for retirement. It should be about helping you to feel better and to enjoy the *whole* of your life.

The programme can open your eyes to the abundance that is all around us, whether it's the kind money can buy directly – or the kind it can't.

Money is part of life and living

Most approaches to budgeting are purely mechanistic – they start off by looking at how much we've got and discuss how we can meet our needs with it. A holistic approach takes many more subtle considerations into account.

We call our programme "holistic" because people are holistic. We are all simultaneously physical, emotional and spiritual beings, whether or not we happen to believe in a god. All these three aspects need to be nourished and nurtured. Physically, we need food, clothing and shelter. Emotionally, we need satisfactory relationships with those close to us. Spiritually, we look to cultural or religious activities.

None of these needs can be met without impacting on the other aspects of our being. Without food and drink we cannot survive – that's the physical aspect. This basic need for survival also influences our emotional needs, especially our need to feel safe, nurtured and cared for. This in turn affects our spiritual well-being, depending on who or what we see as the source of our food and nurturing.

In almost all cultures clothing is much more than protection for our bodies. Almost universally, it is supplemented by some form of adornment to make us feel good about ourselves and make a statement of our status within our social environment. Culture or religion usually dictate how we clothe ourselves.

Housing protects us from the physical environment and gives us privacy. And a home can be a source of beauty that nourishes the spirit.

First, identify your needs

Sanni Kruger worked for many years in charity fundraising, where she learned that every charity exists because it has identified a need or problem and found a way to meet it. The challenge is to find the money to make it happen. Holistic Money Manager works on the same principle, by helping you identify your needs, see how they can be met, and then look at how to find the means to meet them.

One important aspect in this programme is to let go of preconceived ideas about where money comes from. For most of us, work is the principal source of our income. Therefore it is easy to think of it as the *only* source, and imagine that to get more money we simply need to work harder.

The money waterfall

Before you go any further, we invite you to sit down and do a short visualisation exercise. It's important that you do this, because we'll be referring back to it later. You don't have to close your eyes or sit cross-legged – just allow yourself to daydream.

Imagine you are walking through a forest in a mountainous region. Your path leads you along a little stream, busily running its course over a rocky bed. You walk upstream until you find yourself at a waterfall. The path has led you to a point halfway up it, which gives you a clear view of the waterfall and the pool at its foot.

Now look at the mist of spray which is nourishing lichen growing on the rocks all around the waterfall, and the rocky pools around the main basin where water is swirling in and out. The smaller pools near the main basin constantly fill up and empty. The larger ones at the back need longer to fill up but don't seem to fully empty out either – they just overflow sometimes. Most of the water, though, flows straight out of the main basin into the stream.

From where you're standing you can't see exactly where the water is coming from; it could be from a single mighty river, it could be from a number of streams converging, there could even be a reservoir of some kind up there. The source is not important – what is important is the way the water keeps coming.

It's the same with money. **We need to let go of preconceived ideas about where our money should be coming from and focus on the flow.**

Like the river, which never tries to draw its water faster than the water can flow, we need to live within our means. We must learn to accept and use what comes, rather than try to take what we want and let tomorrow look after itself.

Starting your journey

This programme is also different from other budgeting approaches because we give you exercises which will help you to identify a vision for your life, as well as its purpose, and understand how they affect your financial situation. Once you have identified them, book-keeping procedures provide signposts and landmarks to help you to figure out where you are on this journey into the unknown called "life".

If you've glanced ahead, you will have noticed there are a lot of tables with numbers coming up. Most people's first reaction to tables of numbers is to switch off and look for the next page of text. Even accountants do it!

But the tables are there for good reasons. We suggest that when you find yourself doing this, you put the book down for a little while and come back later. Then try to look at the numbers line by line in the light of the preceding explanations and see if they tell you something. Do this for as long as you are comfortable. When you find that you are switching off, walk away from it again for a while. The important thing is that you keep coming back; each time you do so you will find it easier to understand.

CHAPTER 1

Getting a grip on your finances

Working out what you really need and want in life will enable you to do two important things. First, you'll be able to start living within your means. Second, you'll be able to stop spending money you don't have on things you don't need to impress people you don't like – the classic "keeping up with the Joneses" scenario. Third and most important, you'll be able to use your money for the things that are most likely to make you feel fulfilled, secure and happy.

But first, we need to take some practical steps.

Step 1: Write down what you're spending

Start by finding out exactly where and how you spend your money. Buy yourself a little notebook or cashbook and write down *exactly* what you are spending and on what (or track it by some other means, like your mobile phone). You might also want to write down how you spent it – i.e. cash, debit/credit cards, cheques, transfers, automatic payments. Leave a blank column in front of each entry. We will tell you later what this is for. You also need to write down all the money that comes in – how much, where it is coming from and how it is coming in.

How can you be sure that you are taking account of *every* penny, literally? It's easy with bank and debit/credit card payments, because you have the statements to help you. With cash we suggest you count how much you have in your pocket, purse or wallet and write it down in a second little cashbook which you carry around with you at all times. Whenever you spend any cash, ask for a receipt. If no receipt is available, note it down in your book the minute you walk away from the till. You could also use the functions on your mobile phone for this.

When you get home, go through the receipts, or use the entries you've made, write down in your book what you spent the money on, and deduct that from the sum you set out with. Then count your money again to see if this tallies. If not, try to retrace your steps in your mind to find out what you might have done with the missing cash. If you've drawn money from the bank, make sure you add it in your cash book and deduct it from your bank balance.

If you forget to record your transactions, don't try to do it from memory unless you can easily reconstruct it. Instead, start afresh. Carry on until you have at least 4 weeks, or one month, of unbroken records; 6-8 weeks or two months is even better.

Remember that this is a fact-finding exercise. Therefore it is vital that you *do not change your spending habits* for the period in question. Nobody is going to judge you except you yourself.

If you keep forgetting to maintain your books and have to keep starting afresh, it doesn't mean there is something wrong with you. Be patient with yourself. You are learning a completely new way of dealing with money.

This new way is likely to challenge, even shatter, all your entrenched beliefs about money. Many of these are likely to be buried in your subconscious. If you start delving into them you might find that what you think you believe and what you actually believe are two different things.

It may seem easier to stay vague, and your subconscious might sabotage you in unexpected ways. That's when you need to be gentle, but firm, with yourself and simply start again. Eventually you will succeed, and the result will be a coherent record of your income and expenditure.

We usually tell our clients to think of it like the washing up. If you do it straight away, it takes only a few minutes. If you leave it, the stack in the sink gets bigger and bigger, and so does the chore. Every time you look at it you feel that it's too much to tackle right now. You start pulling out the items you need, rinse them and use them. But you are not really sure any more where everything in the kitchen is. You've lost your clarity – and you feel like a slob.

Once you've got into the habit of recording your money inflows and outflows, keep it up – just as you would make an effort to keep up with the washing-up on an ongoing basis.

It will give you much greater clarity about where your money is going. That in turn will give you a pretty good idea what your needs are. If you've tracked your income as well, you also have clarity about how much is coming in and where from. With clarity comes choice, and choice gives you prosperity.

CLARITY → CHOICE → PROSPERITY

Step 2: Categorise and prioritise

Once you have a coherent record of at least 4 weeks or 1 month of your income and expenditure, you need to put it into categories. That's easier said than done, and will need some reflection. On the one hand you want to keep it as simple as possible, yet on the other hand your categories need to be detailed enough to tell you what you need to know.

You might also want to prioritise your categories. For instance, is it more important to you to have a roof over your head than food in your belly? Or are your children or pets more important? We know some people who would rather be homeless and hungry than be without a pet. What is **your** top priority? And the one after that? And the one after that?

We will come back to those priorities later on. For now, they simply help us to categorise our spending. We suggest you go back through your spending records and as you categorise the various entries, create codes for each category.

Create main and sub-categories. For instance, if you decided that food is your top priority then you would make food & drink your category 1. You might then give groceries the code 1A. Now you have that category, go through your spending record and every time you come across a grocery item pencil in code 1A in the column we asked you to keep empty. Then add up these entries and write on a blank sheet of paper:

1.	Food & Drink	
1A	Groceries	xxx

We recommend that you round all the numbers up or down – so any sum between 123.01 and 123.49 becomes 123, and any sum between 123.50 and 123.99 becomes 124. It makes life a lot easier.

Then you need to start thinking. Where do you put snacks and drinks you buy when you are out and about? And what about take-away and restaurant meals? Or meals you buy for someone else? Should they come under "Food" or another main category for "Entertainment"?

We don't want to give you the answer – you have to decide for yourself. You might want to create a separate sub-category for say "shared meals". If you decide to put this under the main category for Food, your list might now look like this:

1.	Food & Drink	
1A	Groceries	xxx
1B	Snacks & Refreshments	xx
1C	Shared Meals	xx

Your no. 2 category could be Housing, with rent/mortgage payments forming category 2A. Utilities might be 2B. Then you might want to add sub-categories for household supplies and day-to-day home maintenance. Again, you need to start thinking about things like garden supplies. Is the garden your hobby, and would you like to put it into a separate category under a different main category? And what about insurance? Do you want one main category for all your different insurance needs, or would you prefer to add them under different categories?

Category 3 might look like this:

3.	Grooming & Clothing	
3A	Clothing & Accessories	xxx
3B	Toiletries & Make-up	xx
3C	Jewellery	xxx
3D	Hairdresser/Barber/Beautician	xxx

Again you have choices about how detailed you want your record to be, and what to put where. For instance, if you spend a lot on make-up or jewellery you might want to have a separate category, simply to gain clarity on how much you spend. However, if you only buy jewellery and/or make-up occasionally you might want to include it with another category.

Next might be categories for your kids; e.g. clothing, pocket money, activities, tuition, education costs.

Other main categories might be:
- Pets
- Looking after yourself (a popular choice is to call this main category "Mind, Body, Spirit")
- Transport
- Leisure
- Family & friends
- Taxes
- Charitable giving
- Savings/set aside
- Debt repayments

You also need to start categorizing your income. For most people their main income comes from work. That could be a salary, or drawings from a business. For others they may be a pension, state benefits, or an allowance. Whatever your principal source of income is, you might want to give it the category "I.1". If you have any other sources of income, e.g. child support, give them another category.

We encourage all our clients to add two more categories: "Gifts & Grants" and "Misc.". The first of these is useful for the odd occasion when you receive a monetary gift or grant (oddly enough, simply adding the category seems to attract this kind of income). The "Misc" category is for the odd windfall, refunds etc. You could combine these two additional categories into one.

Once you've finished, your list of money inflows and outflows (sticking with the idea that money flows like water) might look like this:

	INFLOWS	
I.1	Salary/Drawings	xxxx
I.2	Child Support/Benefit	xxx
I.3	Gifts & Grants	xx
I.4	Misc.	xx
	TOTAL	yyyy
	OUTFLOWS	
1.	**Food & Drink**	
1A	Groceries	xxx
1B	Snacks & Refreshments	xx
1C	Shared Meals	xx
2.	**Housing**	
2A	Rent/Mortgage	xxx
2B	Household Supplies	xx
2C	Home Maintenance	xx

2D	Garden	xx

3. Grooming & Clothing

3A	Clothing & Accessories	xxx
3B	Toiletries & Make-up	xx
3C	Jewellery	xxx
3D	Hairdresser/Barber/Beautician	xxx

4. Children

4A	Clothing	xxx
4B	Pocket Money	xx
4C	Activities/Toys	xx
4D	Tuition/Education	xxx

5. Insurance

5A	Health	xx
5B	Home	xx
5C	Motor	xx

6. Transport

6A	Tax	xx
6B	Fuel	xx
6C	Car Maintenance	xx
6D	Public Transport	xx
6E	Taxis	xx

7. Health Care

7.A	Doctors/Dentist's fees (co-pay)	xx
7.B	Medication	xx
7.C	Supplements	xx

8. Communication

8.A	Phone & Internet	xx
8.B	Postage & Stationery	xx
8.C	Software & Consumables	xx

9. Entertainment/Social

9.A	Hobbies/Clubs	xx
9.B	Home Entertainment	xx
9.C	Reading	xx
9.D	Events, Cinema, Theatre	xx

10. Pets

10.A	Food	xx
10.B	Toys/Equipment	x
10.C	Grooming	xx
10.D	Vet	xx

11. Mind, Body, Spirit

11.A	Church	xx
11.B	Therapy	xxx

11.C Workshops/Courses	xxx
11.D Massages/Body Work	xxx
12. Taxes & other Obligations	
12.A Income Tax Set-Aside	xxx
12.B Child Maintenance	xxx
13. Debt Repayment	
13.A Overdraft	xx
13.B Credit Cards	xx
13.C Store Cards	xx
13.D Loan	xx
TOTAL	**xyxx**

This list looks quite long and detailed, but it is by no means comprehensive. You may have expenditure which is not included in our example. Add it into whichever category is the most appropriate, or create a new one. Make the list right for you. As you'll see further on, you may be able to simplify it later, so that it becomes less time-consuming.

We have assumed that you have added up your spending totals for the period over which you kept records. If you have a 4-week record, and most of your money comes in monthly, you have a rough idea of how much is coming in and going out in a month. You might want to add a little bit extra in some of the discretionary categories to allow for the fact that the average month is more than 4 weeks.

Discretionary categories are the ones where you have control over how much you spend. In the "Housing" category, for instance, your household supplies are discretionary, but your rent/mortgage is not.

Now that you have a record of your monthly income and expenditure, you have achieved the first step towards the *clarity* which will allow you to ask yourself questions and make meaningful *choices*. You have therefore taken the first major step towards *prosperity*.

Step 3: A question of balance

Next, you need to compare the total figures for inflow and outflow. Does the inflow exceed the outflow? That, of course, is the ideal position. If the outflow exceeds the inflow, however, ask yourself if this was a period of normal spending, or if there was unusually heavy expenditure. If so, can you pinpoint the problem? How likely is it that this will happen again, and when?

If you find that your outflows normally exceed your inflows, you are not living within your means. Strange as this sounds, it is the next piece in the puzzle of the kind of clarity that will give you real choices and ultimately lead you to prosperity. It's important not to beat yourself up over it – just accept it as a fact.

Now you need to learn to live within your means; maybe for the first time in your life. Why is it so important to live within one's means, and why do we get so stressed and feel under pressure if we don't? For us at Holistic Money Manager, it has to do with integrity. We believe that most people are decent and honest by nature. However, if we buy something on credit or with money we have borrowed, i.e. we don't really have, we are one step away from theft. If you don't pay back the money you owe that's what it is, even if it's called something else – like "written off". If you are a self-employed person who has ever had to write off money owed to you, you'll know exactly what we mean.

If you are a decent, honest person, the minute you borrow money you are under pressure to pay it back. The more money you borrow, the greater the pressure becomes. It gets more and more painful to look at bank or credit card statements. Until you reach the point when you don't open the mail…

You may not necessarily **feel** pain or shame about this. But we believe it's there somewhere in your subconscious, making you feel bad. Perhaps you try to deal with these feelings by telling yourself that you're not really hurting anyone, that these big businesses don't need your little bit of money and they'll just write it off. Or perhaps you go out shopping to pretend you are still free to spend, or deal with it some other way.

You might go to the other extreme and put your debt repayments before your needs. That is likely to put you in what we call the "debt spiral"; where the minimum repayments cripple you to such an extent that it is impossible to make ends meet. So you have to incur more debt simply to make it from payday to payday.

Whatever you do, you are likely to end up feeling guilty, stressed and worried. The whole vicious circle keeps merrily going around, eventually spiralling out of control. For some people it may get so bad that they actually contemplate, attempt or even commit suicide.

That's why learning to live within your means is so vital. It can be a huge change, and it may take some time to achieve. But you **can do it**.

How? The answer lies in planning. Some people call it budgeting, but we prefer to use the term **cashflow planning**.

CHAPTER 2

Using cashflow planning to build your wealth

The word "budget" immediately conjures up associations of restraint, rigidity, self-denial – even deprivation. It has a tendency to make us feel bad about our spending habits. You might be tempted towards rebellion, to thoughts of "What the heck!". Then, before you know it, you are back in the vicious circle of spending money to make yourself feel better.

Cashflow planning is much more fluid and flexible. It allows you to start again at any point, shift things around and generally feel more positive about your money.

We have noticed something curious about using cashflow plans to live within your means: It somehow brings more money into our lives. We don't quite know how it works, but work it does. It starts off with the very real sense of prosperity that cashflow planning brings about and ends up with actual money in the bank; with a gradual increase in savings (both for long and short term purposes) and a simultaneous decrease in debts.

Your spending record is your starting point for making a cashflow plan. However, keeping up a list as detailed as the one above would be a lot of hard work in the long term. We have given you this example to help you to remember to include everything you might possibly spend money on. Once you have the necessary clarity about your needs and where and how you want to spend your money, it's helpful to simplify. How you do that depends on your particular circumstances and the level of clarity you need so that you can feel in control of your finances.

First, you need to decide how far in advance you want to plan. We advise you not to go beyond one month, and to base your plan on the intervals at which you receive your principal income. Most people are paid monthly and most major outflows, such as rent/mortgage payments and regular bills, are also paid monthly. That's why we base the examples we give on one month. If however your income is irregular – if you are self-employed, for example, and get paid on a project basis – you may find that a three-month period is more useful.

Now to the practical bits. You can either use a spreadsheet, or work with pen & paper. Both methods have their advantages. Spreadsheets allow you to calculate very quickly and allow you to run through "what if" scenarios. On the other hand, if you use pen & paper you can keep track of your finances without having to switch on your computer first. Or you might want to use a combination of the two – e.g. spreadsheets for your cashflow plan and pen & paper for your daily record keeping.

In the following examples we assume that you have opted for the pen & paper method. We recommend that you buy a "cash analysis book" with 3 columns (sometimes called a triple cash book). These can be quite expensive, and you might be tempted to think that a simple exercise book in which you will draw the columns will do. Actually it won't – it's the perfect way to set yourself up for failure. Trust us on this one and invest in a prosperous life!

We also recommend that you use a pencil, rather than a pen. That helps you to correct mistakes you make or to make changes, as and when they are needed. More about that later.

Now to drawing up your plan. The first thing to enter is your income. We recommend that you start your cashflow plan just after you receive your main income. For instance if you are paid at the end of the month, start on the 1st day of the following one. If you are paid on the 15th of the month, start on the 16th. (We will deal with situations where you are paid weekly or fortnightly later.)

You start off with your inflows:

Sept		Plan	Received	Outstanding
INFLOWS				
I.1	Salary/Drawings (Aug.)	1,658	1,658.23	0
I.2	Child Support, Benefit (Aug.)	321	320.57	0
I.3	Gifts & Grants			
I.4	Misc	34		34
	TOTAL	**2,013**	**1,978.80**	34

We assume that you have been paid 1,658.23 at the end of August. (If tax has been deducted by your employer you don't need to worry about it any further. If this is your gross pay you have to set aside money for your taxes. We'll show you how.) We also assume that you received the sum of 320.57 in either child support or benefit at some time in August.

If you have already spent some of the money you received in August, add up how much you actually have left on the first day in September. Put the full amount in the "Received" column, but round either up or down to the nearest full number in the "Plan" column. Since you have actually received what you planned to receive, there is no money outstanding and therefore you put a "0" in the "Outstanding" column.

In this example we also assume that you have received a refund of £33.99 for an item you returned to a mail order company, but you have not been able to deposit the cheque into the bank yet. Therefore we added "34" in the "Plan" column under "I.4 Misc." However, since you haven't actually paid in the money you leave the "Received" column blank. Still, you add it to the total amount available for spending in September.

Now we start looking at your money outflows. Most of our clients find it easiest to make a list of all their non-discretionary and/or regular spending. If you use a spreadsheet you could either incorporate this list into your worksheet or use a separate one, whichever you find easier. If you use pen and paper we suggest that you keep this list separate but somewhere in the book, perhaps the inside cover or front or back sheet. We also suggest that you use a pencil so that you can amend the details and/or rectify mistakes.

Your list could look like this:

What	Amount	Who to	How	Notes
Taxes	331.60	HMRC	Automated Payment	
Mortgage	125.23	Megabank	Automated Payment	
Health Insurance	35.64	Insurance Co Ltd	Automated Payment	
Landline/ISP	18.58	Interphone	Automated Payment	
Mobile/Cell	35.00	Roamaphone	Automated Payment	
Pension	74.90	Saveco Pensions	Automated Payment	
TOTAL	**620.95**			

We usually recommend that you create a "buffer" to allow for price increases. You can do this by rounding **up** to the nearest full number or even the nearest £5. If you have a bank overdraft it's also a neat way to reduce the overdraft slowly and steadily without really missing the money.

Let's assume you decided to round up to the nearest 5. Your list now looks like this:

What	Amount	Who to	How	Notes
Taxes	331.60	HMRC	Automated Payment	
Mortgage	125.23	Megabank	Automated Payment	
Health Insurance	35.64	Insurance Co Ltd	Automated Payment	
Landline/ISP	18.58	Interphone	Automated Payment	
Mobile/Cell	35.00	Roamaphone	Automated Payment	
Pension	74.90	Saveco Pensions	Automated Payment	
TOTAL	620.95			
Buffer	4.05			
TOTAL	**625.00**			

You now have another list of set-aside categories for your periodic outflows. It might look like this:

What	Amount	Who to	How	How often
Electricity	14.00	Big Electric Co	Automated Payment	quarterly
Gas	19.00	Big Gas Inc.	Automated Payment	quarterly
Water & Sewage	24.00	Local Authority	Automated Payment	quarterly
Dental check-ups	11.00	Dental Clinic	Debit card in person	6-monthly
Car Tax	10.00	Licensing Authority	Cheque at Post office	6-monthly
Anti-virus software	6.00	Big AV Company	Debit card online	annually
Magazine subs	12.00	Famous Mag.	Cheque on invoice	annually
Health Club	38.00	Big Health Club	Debit card online	annually
TOTAL	**134.00**			

Now your cashflow plan now looks like this:

Sept		Plan	Received	Outstanding
	INFLOWS			
I.1	Salary/Drawings (Aug.)	1,658	1,658.23	0
I.2	Child Support, Benefit (Aug.)	321	320.57	0
I.3	Gifts & Grants			
I.4	Misc	34		34
	TOTAL	2,013	1,978.80	
	OUTFLOWS	**Plan**	**Spent/Act**	**Remaining**
AP	Auto Payments	625	625.00	0
PP	Periodic Payments	134	134.00	0

You don't actually do anything with this money. It just stays in the bank account, ready to be used as and when the bill arrives. This approach is another method of reducing stress and anxiety about your finances, because now you *know* that you have sufficient cash in the bank to pay your bills.

Again you enter the whole amount you are setting aside for Periodic Payments in the "Spent" column, with "0" in the "Remaining" one.

At this point you may want to add another line for regular savings allowances. For instance, instead of spending the allocated amount for "Clothing & Accessories" and/or "Jewellery" in the same month you might want to put the money into

You now have another list of set-aside categories for your periodic outflows. It might look like this:

What	Amount	Who to	How	How often
Electricity	14.00	Big Electric Co	Automated Payment	quarterly
Gas	19.00	Big Gas Inc.	Automated Payment	quarterly
Water & Sewage	24.00	Local Authority	Automated Payment	quarterly
Dental check-ups	11.00	Dental Clinic	Debit card in person	6-monthly
Car Tax	10.00	Licensing Authority	Cheque at Post office	6-monthly
Anti-virus software	6.00	Big AV Company	Debit card online	annually
Magazine subs	12.00	Famous Mag.	Cheque on invoice	annually
Health Club	38.00	Big Health Club	Debit card online	annually
TOTAL	**134.00**			

Now your cashflow plan now looks like this:

Sept		Plan	Received	Outstanding
	INFLOWS			
I.1	Salary/Drawings (Aug.)	1,658	1,658.23	0
I.2	Child Support, Benefit (Aug.)	321	320.57	0
I.3	Gifts & Grants			
I.4	Misc	34		34
	TOTAL	2,013	1,978.80	
	OUTFLOWS	**Plan**	**Spent/Act**	**Remaining**
AP	Auto Payments	625	625.00	0
PP	Periodic Payments	134	134.00	0

You don't actually do anything with this money. It just stays in the bank account, ready to be used as and when the bill arrives. This approach is another method of reducing stress and anxiety about your finances, because now you *know* that you have sufficient cash in the bank to pay your bills.

Again you enter the whole amount you are setting aside for Periodic Payments in the "Spent" column, with "0" in the "Remaining" one.

At this point you may want to add another line for regular savings allowances. For instance, instead of spending the allocated amount for "Clothing & Accessories" and/or "Jewellery" in the same month you might want to put the money into a savings account so that you can use it to buy more expensive items from time to time. Similarly you might want to put some money aside each month for major celebrations which occur annually, such as Christmas. Some of our clients with large families also put money aside each month for their summer holiday and/or family outings.

Your list could look like this:

What	Amount	Where to
Clothing & Accessories	50	Clothing Fund
Christmas	45	Special Purpose Savings
Summer Holiday	45	Special Purpose Savings
TOTAL	**140**	

As with earlier regular payments and set aside amounts for periodic payments you might want to list each of them in a separate worksheet of your cashflow plan spreadsheet or, if you work with pen and paper, create a third list.

Your cashflow plan would then look like this:

Sept		Plan	Received	Outstanding
	INFLOWS			
I.1	Salary/Drawings (Aug.)	1,658	1,658.23	0
I.2	Child Support, Benefit (Aug.)	321	320.57	0
I.3	Gifts & Grants			
I.4	Misc	34		34
	TOTAL	2,013	1,978.80	
	OUTFLOWS	**Plan**	**Spent/Act**	**Remaining**
AP	Auto Payments	625	625.00	0
PP	Periodic Payments	134	134.00	0
SP	Special Purpose Savings	140		140
	Sub-Total	**899**	**759.00**	

We suggest that you transfer the money to your Special Purpose Savings account(s) as soon as possible. In our example we assume that you have not yet done it. Therefore the "Spent" column is left empty and "140" entered in the "Remaining" column.

Now you deduct that sub-total from your total income, which gives you £1,114 to spend on your discretionary categories. Here's your cashflow plan:

Sept		Plan	Received	Outstanding
	INFLOWS			
I.1	Salary/Drawings (Aug.)	1,658	1,658.23	0
I.2	Child Support, Benefit (Aug.)	321	320.57	0
I.3	Gifts & Grants			
I.4	Misc	34		34
	TOTAL	2,013	1,978.80	
	OUTFLOWS	Plan	Spent/Act	Remaining
AP	Auto Payments	625	625.00	0
PP	Periodic Payments	134	134.00	0
SP	Special Purpose Savings	140		140
	Sub-Total	899	759.00	
	TOTAL AVAILABLE	1,114	1,219.80	

Now you have taken care of all your regular outgoings and money you want to set aside, you are left with a sum of money for your discretionary (day-to-day) spending. In our example it is £1,114.

Many of the outflow categories from your spending record will be taken care of by now. At this point many of our clients simplify their spending categories by combining sub categories. Some leave only main categories.

Now you go back to your totals in your spending record and work out how much you are likely to spend in a month. If you have kept records for 4 weeks you could simply use that total and enter it in your "Plan" column as the amount you plan to spend in a month. If you have kept records for longer than 4 weeks you could divide the total in each category by the number of weeks you kept records for, multiply the result by 52 and then divide by 12.

Unfortunately both these methods are likely to leave you short, as the year never has exactly 52 weeks. For example, let's assume that you kept records for 4 weeks (28 days). In that time you spent £225.53 on "Groceries & Supplies". You could simply enter "226" as your planned spending for the month of September. A more accurate formula goes like this: Divide 225.53 by 28. Then multiply by 365 and divide by 12:

$$225.53 \div 28 = 8.05; \quad 8.05 \times 365 = 2,938.25; \quad 2,938.25 \div 12 = 244.85$$

As you can see, the difference between your two figures is nearly £19. Now repeat this process with each of your categories. It may seem a lot of hard work, but it gives you a solid foundation on which to build on. And you only need to go through this detailed process once, because if you continue to work with a cashflow plan and monitor it, you always have the clear, accurate data you need to make informed choices.

That's what this programme is all about: having the clarity to make meaningful choices. *No matter how little money you may have at the start, having real choices will begin to give you a sense of prosperity.*

Now back to your plan. In our example it looks like this:

Sept		Plan	Received	Outstanding
	INFLOWS			
I.1	Salary/Drawings (Aug.)	1,658	1,658.23	0
I.2	Child Support, Benefit (Aug.)	321	320.57	0
I.3	Gifts & Grants			
I.4	Misc	34		34
	TOTAL	2,013	1,978.80	
	OUTFLOWS	**Plan**	**Spent/Act**	**Remaining**
AP	Auto Payments	625	625.00	0
PP	Periodic Payments	134	134.00	0
SP	Special Purpose Savings	140		140
	Sub-Total	899	759.00	
	TOTAL AVAILABLE	1,114	1,219.80	
	Day-to-Day			
1	**Household**			
1.A	Groceries & Supplies	245		
1.B	Children	185		
1.C	Pets & Garden	40		
1.D	Eat Out & Take Away Meals	55		
2.	**Personal Care**			
2.A	Grooming/Make-up	62		
2.B	Health Care	34		
2.C	Body Work	45		
3.	**Transport**			
3.A	Car	95		
3.B	Public Transport & Taxis	15		
4.	**Communication**			
4.A	Postage, Stationery Consumables	41		
4.B	Reference Books & Mags.	26		
5.	**Leisure, Friends & Family**			
5.A	Hobbies	63		
5.B	Entertainment/Fiction	112		
5.C	Outings	165		
5.D	Gifts etc.	45		
	TOTAL	1,228		

As you can see, the planned spending exceeds the available money. So now you go back over your spending record. Were there any categories where the expenditure was unusually high? If so could it be reduced, and if so by how much?

If these figures are your usual spending, where can you reduce it? The aim is that your planned total day-to-day outflows come to £1,114, or preferably less. In the above example you need to "lose" £114. For instance, you could decide to postpone a planned outing to an attraction to another month and go somewhere else instead which costs less. We assume that would reduce this category by £48 to £117. That leaves you with another £66 to "lose". Let's say you think you could reduce the groceries category by £20, to the £225 you spent over 4 weeks. Now you continue the process until your cashflow plan looks like this:

Sept		Plan	Received	Outstanding
	INFLOWS			
I.1	Salary/Drawings (Aug.)	1,658	1,658.23	0
I.2	Child Support, Benefit (Aug.)	321	320.57	0
I.3	Gifts & Grants			
I.4	Misc	34		34
	TOTAL	2,013	1,978.80	
	OUTFLOWS	**Plan**	**Spent/Act**	**Remaining**
AP	Auto Payments	625	625.00	0
PP	Periodic Payments	134	134.00	0
SP	Special Purpose Savings	140		140
	Sub-Total	899	759.00	
	TOTAL AVAILABLE	1,114	1,219.80	
	Day-to-Day			
1.	**Household**			
1.A	Groceries & Supplies	225		
1.B	Children	185		
1.C	Pets & Garden	36		
1.D	Eat Out & Take Away Meals	40		
2.	**Personal Care**			
2.A	Grooming/Make-up	62		
2.B	Health Care	34		
2.C	Body Work	45		
3.	**Transport**			
3.A	Car	80		
3.B	Public Transport & Taxis	15		
4.	**Communication**			
4.A	Postage, Stationery Consumables	41		
4.B	Reference Books & Mags.	22		
5.	**Leisure, Friends & Family**			
5.A	Hobbies	60		
5.B	Entertainment/Fiction	112		
5.C	Outings	117		
5.D	Gifts etc.	40		
	TOTAL	1,114		

If you use a spreadsheet the formulae should look like this (for the sake of clarity we've left out the numbers):

	A	B	C	D	E
1	Sept		Plan	Received	Outstanding
2		**INFLOWS**			
3	I.1	Salary/Drawings (Aug.)			=D3-C3
4	I.2	Child Support, Benefit (Aug.)			=D4-C4
5	I.3	Gifts & Grants			=D5-C5
6	I.4	Misc.			=D6-C6
7		TOTAL	=SUM(C3:C6)	=SUM(D3:D6)	
8		**OUTFLOWS**	**Plan**	**Spent/Act**	**Remaining**
9	AP	Auto Payments			=C9-D9
10	PP	Periodic Payments			=C10-D10
11	SP	Special Purpose Savings			=C11-D11
12		Sub-Total	=SUM(C9:C11)	=SUM(D9:D11)	
13		TOTAL AVAILABLE	=C7-C12	=D7-D12	
14		**Day-to-Day**			
15	**1.**	**Household**			
16	1.A	Groceries & Supplies			
17	1.B	Children			
18	1.C	Pets & Garden			
19	1.D	Eat Out & Take Away Meals			
20	**2.**	**Personal Care**			
21	2.A	Grooming/Make-up			
22	2.B	Health Care			
23	2.C	Body Work			
24	**3.**	**Transport**			
25	3.A	Car			
26	3.B	Public Transport & Taxis			
27	**4.**	**Communication**			
28	4.A	Postage, Stationery, Consumables			
29	4.B	Reference Books & Mags.			
30	**5.**	**Leisure, Friends & Family**			
31	5.A	Hobbies			
32	5.B	Entertainment/Fiction			
33	5.C	Outings			
34	5.D	Gifts etc.			
35		TOTAL	=SUM(C16:C34)	=Sum(D16:D34)	

So there you have it – a working plan. ***Congratulations! You have made the first real big progress towards living within your means.***

CHAPTER 3

Getting on top of debt
The stranger in the shadows

So many of us fail to use debt properly. The result is that it gets out of control – slightly, or horribly. It becomes the ogre under the bed, the stranger lurking in the shadows who just won't go away, the nagging voice that wakes us in the middle of the night.

Not all debt is bad – some is necessary, if for example we want to buy our own home and don't happen to be rich enough to pay for it in cash. But there's no doubt that getting rid of debt is one of the most important steps you can take in getting on better terms with money.

You may already be trapped in a "debt spiral". It works like this: The minimum payments on your credit cards are so high that you are left with too little money to meet your expenses. Therefore, you need to incur more debt on the cards simply to get by. The next month your minimum payment(s) have increased – and so on and so on, as the debt mounts you become more and more worried.

If you get into this position, it may well be time to start negotiating with your creditors. You might need to use a debt counselling service, such as the Consumer Credit Counselling Service or the Citizen's Advice Bureau (in Britain) to do it on your behalf.

This is especially important if you have "priority debt" – that means any debt that could either land you in prison or make you homeless. For instance, if you owe taxes or fines you could eventually go to jail. If you get behind with mortgage or rent payments your home could be repossessed by the lender/landlord. Some people also class arrears of utility bills as priority debt, because the service will be discontinued if you don't pay within a certain length of time.

The debt counselling service will help you to identify your priority debt, and create a budget for you. You then have the option to use it as it stands as the basis for your cashflow plan, or adapt it more in line with your real needs.

You should also make a distinction between secured and unsecured debt. It is usually the unsecured debt that causes us the most stress. A secured debt is usually secured against some form of asset, the "collateral". In most cases the collateral is a property. Therefore a mortgage is a secured debt. If you buy a car under a finance agreement, then the car is the collateral. This is another secured debt. You can sum up a secured debt with the saying: "If I don't keep up the repayments, the asset will be taken away from me."

Any debt not secured against some form of collateral is unsecured. This includes your credit cards, store cards and bank overdraft. Some people mistakenly believe that their cards are secured against their property. Yes, you may end up losing your home, for instance, if you are declared bankrupt, but legally credit card debt etc is unsecured.

Since it is the unsecured debt that gets us into trouble, it's usually this kind we are talking about when we talk about "debt" in this programme. We also include any arrears of mortgage payments and finance deal instalments. We strongly recommend that you make a firm commitment to yourself not to incur ANY new unsecured debt.

In order to do that, you might need to cut up your credit and/or store cards, and cancel your overdraft facility. This is a huge step to take. You may want somebody to sit with you and support you while you do it.

We know that we can only achieve some things in our lives by incurring some form of secured debt. Buying a house, for instance, comes under that category. So might be buying a decent vehicle to get around in. Or if you are setting up in business, you may need a cash injection to get going. In this case you might want to investigate "asset finance", specialist lenders who will secure a loan against some essential equipment of your venture.

If you work with this programme you will very soon be in a position to make real informed decisions about how to finance your dreams and visions with a minimum of liabilities.

We firmly believe that your needs come before those of your creditors, so we always put debt repayments at the bottom of any cashflow plan. In a little while we'll also give you an additional or alternative debt repayment strategy.

For the moment let's assume that you have negotiated a monthly payment of £10 each to three of your creditors. Once you have made that commitment you really need to demonstrate to your creditors that you are serious about repaying your debts. For that reason we strongly recommend that you set up automated payments to them. In our example the list of automated payments changes accordingly to this:

What	Amount	Who to	How	Notes
Taxes (current)	331.60	HMRC	Automated Payment	
Mortgage	125.23	Megabank	Automated Payment	
Health Insurance	35.64	Insurance Co Ltd	Automated Payment	
Landline/ISP	18.58	Interphone	Automated Payment	
Mobile/Cell	35.00	Roamaphone	Automated Payment	
Pension	74.90	Saveco Pensions	Automated Payment	
Mortgage Arrerars	10.00	Megabank	Automated Payment	
Back Taxes	10.00	HMRC	Automated Payment	
Credit Card	10.00	CC Co	Automated Payment	
TOTAL	650.95			
Buffer	4.05			
TOTAL	**655.00**			

And the cashflow plan looks like this (we've highlighted the numbers which have changed):

Sept		Plan	Received	Outstanding
	INFLOWS			
I.1	Salary/Drawings (Aug.)	1,658	1,658.23	0
I.2	Child Support, Benefit (Aug.)	321	320.57	0
I.3	Gifts & Grants			
I.4	Misc	34		34
	TOTAL	2,013	1,978.80	
	OUTFLOWS	**Plan**	**Spent/Act**	**Remaining**
AP	Auto Payments	655	655.00	0
PP	Periodic Payments	134	134.00	0
SP	Special Purpose Savings	140		140
	Sub-Total	929	789.00	
	TOTAL AVAILABLE	1,084	1,189.80	
	Day-to-Day			
1.	**Household**			
1.A	Groceries & Supplies	220		
1.B	Children	180		
1.C	Pets & Garden	36		
1.D	Eat Out & Take Away Meals	40		
2.	**Personal Care**			
2.A	Grooming/Make-up	52		
2.B	Health Care	34		
2.C	Body Work	45		
3.	**Transport**			
3.A	Car	80		
3.B	Public Transport & Taxis	15		
4.	**Communication**			
4.A	Postage, Stationery Consumables	38		
4.B	Reference Books & Mags.	20		
5.	**Leisure, Friends & Family**			
5.A	Hobbies	60		
5.B	Entertainment/Fiction	112		
5.C	Outings	117		
5.D	Gifts etc.	35		
	TOTAL	1,084		

So far, this might not look so very different from any other budgeting programme you have come across. You might feel hemmed in and restricted, even deprived. That's all right. Remember that this is only a short-term measure to help you live within your means. Once you do that consistently, your means *will* expand.

You will have to think about your means in a new way, though. Many people think money is their only means. But what do we need money for? Usually to buy things. But some of these things can come into your life without your having to pay for them. Stephanie was in the debt spiral. She chose to meet the minimum repayments for her various credit cards in full while in the process of restructuring her debt. She was committed to not incurring any new debt and for a whole month had very little cash left to live on. Yet, she found that money came to her during that month in many unexpected ways; and not only money. She would be offered free food and other items by people who were totally unaware of her financial situation.

You don't necessarily have to go to Stephanie's extreme, but you may find that this commitment to not incurring new debt and being open to the abundance of the world will act like a magnet.

Sanni, our principal, tells this story: "There was a time in my life when I had literally no income whatsoever for about three months and had to live off very meagre savings. It was a cold winter, and I desperately needed a warm coat. I was willing to get one from a charity shop, but there simply was nothing suitable available. I looked around the shops and found the coat I wanted, but it cost £80 – a lot of money when there is no money coming in. I sat with this prospect for a few days, full of fear that if I spent that money I would have to go hungry. On the other hand I was desperately cold every time I left the house, filling me with the fear of becoming ill. With a heavy heart I finally went to the bank to withdraw the £80 from my fast dwindling savings account. As I went into the bank I suddenly heard a voice that seemed to come out of nowhere saying: 'Your thinking is limited.' I shrugged my shoulders, withdrew the cash, went to the shop – and found that the price of the coat had been reduced by £10. That is a lot of money when you have no income. The thought that this might happen had simply not occurred to me. So my thinking was limited indeed."

Sanni says she has never forgotten that incident. It opened her consciousness to the idea that she might receive what she needs in any number of different ways. Since then she has never again been in such a difficult situation.

Remember the waterfall? We said that from your position halfway up you could not tell where exactly the water was coming from, only that it kept coming. That's the important point. It will be the same for you, as long as you stick to your commitment not to take on any more unsecured debt. Whenever you are filled with fear, just ask yourself where you might look. If you belong to a faith, you might want to do this in the context of prayer.

Many people also think that work is the only path to money. Many of Sanni's "prosperity gurus" are into rebirthing. We don't know much about rebirthing, but we believe it's a thought system concerned with what happened in the very earliest days of life, around the time of birth, and what conclusions people have reached at that time. We think that if that's true, those conclusions were reached at a non-verbal stage and are now deeply buried within our being at a level beyond our normal, verbal consciousness. At that time of our life nourishment came from one source, and one source only, mother or the bottle. Has that experience led us to the conclusion that now there is only one source of income; i.e. work?

Here's a little exercise that will open your consciousness. Write a list of at least 100 ways in which money could come into your life. The rules are simple: No matter how illegal, immoral, impossible, undesirable – if it occurs to you, write it down.

Your list could look like this:

1. **win the lottery**
2. **ask for a raise**
3. **swindle someone**
4. **inherit a fortune**
5. **get a new job**
6. **open an internet shop**
7. **rob a bank**
8. **write a bestseller (the next Harry Potter)**
9. **prostitution**
10. **?**

Some people find it easy to write this list, while others struggle to get beyond the first 10 items. If that is the case for you, we suggest you leave the sheet of paper lying around or take it with you wherever you go. When another idea occurs to you, add it to the list. It might take you weeks, even months, to get there, but that doesn't really matter. Remember that the important point is to start thinking about where money comes from in a different way. We recommend that you repeat this exercise from time to time.

Now let's talk about the practicalities of how you are going to actually manage your money on a daily basis.

Many of our clients decide to open a second current account. Normally the one they have already is set up to receive their pay etc., and where all the auto payments (direct debits and standing orders) go out of. We suggest that you leave all those arrangements as they are, but that you open a second current account with a cheque book and debit card. Some of our clients give those accounts names. In our example we will call the old account "Pay account" and the new one "D2D account".

Working on the figures we used above, at the beginning of the month you transfer £1,084 from the Pay account to the D2D account. For the rest of the month you use only the D2D account. That way you always know exactly how much money you have left.

Some clients find that almost all their money either goes out automatically or is set aside. All they do on a day-to-day basis is a big weekly shopping trip to the supermarket, with just minor incidental purchases, so they decide to allow themselves a certain sum per week for that. If the people in our example adopted this method, their cashflow plan might look like this:

Sept			Plan	Received	Outstanding
	INFLOWS				
I.1	Salary/Drawings (Aug.)		1,658	1,658.23	0
I.2	Child Support, Benefit (Aug.)		321	320.57	0
I.3	Gifts & Grants				
I.4	Misc		34		34
		TOTAL	2,013	1,978.80	
	OUTFLOWS		Plan	Spent/Act	Remaining
AP	Auto Payments		655	655.00	0
PP	Periodic Payments		134	134.00	0
SP	Special Purpose Savings		140		140
		Sub-Total	929	789.00	
	TOTAL AVAILABLE		1,084	1,189.80	
	Day-to-Day				
	Supermarket (250 per week)		1,000		1,000
	Incidentals (21 per week)		84		84
		TOTAL	1,084		

It doesn't really matter which method you adopt, as long as it works for you; in other words, you find it easy to manage and it tells you how much money you have where for what. You are likely to find that over time the way you manage your money, and keep tabs on it, evolves with your changing awareness and circumstances.

So how exactly do you keep tabs? You need two books – one to record your transactions and the other one, the one we've described above, to monitor what's actually happening against the plan.

You could simply continue with the same book you used for your initial spending record to record your transactions. However, we recommend that you buy a second cash analysis book. The number of columns you need depends on how many current accounts you run. If you follow our example you'll need another book with 3 columns (triple cash book). The columns are headed "Cash", "D2D account" and "Pay account".

			Cash	D2D account	Pay account
31.8.11	Balance		0.00	0.00	1,978.80
1.9.11	From Pay a/c	xfer		+1,084.00	-1,084.00

This enables you to see at once what's been happening, as well as telling you how much money you have and where. In this example we start on the assumption that you have absolutely no cash in your pocket, and that you're opening your new day-to-day account with a transfer of £1,084 from your old account, the one we now call the "Pay account". We also assume that in the Pay account you have only the money that came in during August.

That is highly unlikely to happen in the real world. Let's assume that you had £4.68 cash left in your pocket and £3.01 in your old current account, the one we now call "Pay account". That makes £7.69 in total.

We suggest that from now on you adopt a system that you use for any surplus money or windfalls: you divide the money by 3. In this case it would make two parts of £2.56 and one of £2.57. However, as we tend to use only full numbers in our plan, we suggest that you round the money you have brought forward down to the nearest whole number; i.e. £7. Therefore you would have two parts of £2 and one of £3.

The first part you use to treat yourself with something you might think of as frivolous, such as a glossy magazine. The second part you save in a contingency fund, and the third one you use towards debt repayment.

These amounts may seem too trifling to bother with, but doing this will get you out of the "all or nothing" habit. If you follow our recommendation you are likely to feel good about yourself, while if you use all of it for one purpose you might well end up feeling uncomfortable. Why?

Let's say you decided to spend the whole £7 to treat yourself. You are very likely to feel guilty. If on the other hand you put all the cash into your contingency fund, you might feel resentful. And if you put all the money towards debt repayment, you are prone to feel deprived (which might then tempt you to go on a spending spree).

We believe it is very important for people to learn to treat themselves well. For too long we might have tried to punish ourselves for being in debt by depriving ourselves. Or we may have been so scared of getting into debt that we have hoarded money but denied ourselves any pleasure that involves parting with cash.

A contingency fund is the most important measure you can introduce into your money management, because it stands between you and new debt. This is the money that could keep you afloat if you were to lose your job or unable to generate income due to another reason, such as illness, bereavement etc. For this reason it is generally recommended that employees need to build up a fund of 3-6 months living costs, and self-employed people/business owners 6-9 months.

 If you have negotiated a debt repayment plan with your creditors you may be unwilling to make any extra payments, because it might make them think that you can now afford to pay them more. In this case we recommend that you put the money for debt repayment into a separate savings account until you are able to make a larger one-off lump-sum payment.

Your cashflow plan would now look like this:

Sept		Plan	Received	Outstanding
INFLOWS				
I.1	Salary/Drawings (Aug.)	1,658	1,658.23	0
I.2	Child Support, Benefit (Aug.)	321	320.57	0
I.3	Gifts & Grants			
I.4	Misc.	34		34
	TOTAL	2,013	1,978.80	
OUTFLOWS		**Plan**	**Spent/Act**	**Remaining**
AP	Auto Payments	655	655.00	0
PP	Periodic Payments	134	134.00	0
SP	Special Purpose Savings	140		140
	Sub-Total	929	789.00	
	TOTAL AVAILABLE	1,084	1,189.80	
	Day-to-Day			
1.	**Household**			
1.A	Groceries & Supplies	220		220
1.B	Children	180		180
1.C	Pets & Garden	36		36
1.D	Eat Out & Take Away Meals	40		40
2.	**Personal Care**			
2.A	Grooming/Make-up	52		52
2.B	Health Care	34		34
2.C	Body Work	45		45
3.	**Transport**			
3.A	Car	80		80
3.B	Public Transport & Taxis	15		15
4.	**Communication**			
4.A	Postage, Stationery, Consumables	38		38
4.B	Reference Books & Mags.	20		20
5.	**Leisure, Friends & Family**			
5.A	Hobbies	60		60
5.B	Entertainment/Fiction	112		112
5.C	Outings	117		117
5.D	Gifts etc.	35		35
	TOTAL	**1,084**		
	Surplus	*0*		
	Brought forward	*7*		
	TOTAL SURPLUS	**7**		
	Frivolity	*2*		*2*
	Contingency	*2*		*2*
	Debt Repayment	*3*		*3*
	TOTAL	**7**		

Your daily bookkeeping book now looks like this:

		Cash	D2D account	Pay account
31.8.11	Balance	4.68	0.00	3.01
1.2	Child Support, benefit (Aug.)			+320.57
1.1	Salary/Drawings (Aug.)			+1,658.23
1.9.11	Balance			1,981.81
	From Pay a/c	xfer	+1,084.00	-1,084.00

Did you notice in the cashflow plan that we inserted a line saying "Surplus" above the "brought forward" row? That is simply because sooner or later you will come to the point in drawing up your spending plan when, after you have taken care of all your needs and deducted the total from the money available, there WILL be a surplus.

You will also find that the longer you practise this way of managing your money, the more often you are left with money at the end of the month without quite knowing how it happened. That is what we mean by saying that once you learn to live within your means, your means expand.

As we did in our example, we suggest you add the surplus to the cash brought forward and then divide the sum by 3 and allocate it as described above.

Treating Ourselves

Do you remember that right at the very beginning we said that this programme is not about tightening belts and wearing hair shirts? The purpose of this programme is not to make you "save" money. It's about learning to live within your means. For this reason it's important to bring comfort into your life and allow room to treat yourself.

We have called the category in the cashflow plan "Frivolity". Some of our clients call it "Fiscal Fun", others "Extravagance", yet others "Indulgence". It doesn't really matter what you call it, as long as you understand that this money is for you.

Likewise, what you spend that money on should itself make you feel good. Usually it's something you wouldn't include in your normal day-to-day spending; a treat of some sort. You have to decide for yourself what that might be. Something that you regard as an occasional treat might be part of normal expenditure for others, and vice versa.

Some of our clients decide not to spend the money in their "Frivolity" category immediately but to save up for something special. Sheila loves certain singers and belongs to a number of fan clubs. The subscriptions for these clubs come out of her day-to-day spending. In addition she saves her "Frivolity" money for concerts. She usually has enough money to go for the V.I.P. option. That often includes things like backstage tours, meeting the star, or pre-show meals. Do you get the idea?

The Contingency Fund

We said that your contingency fund could keep you afloat if you were to lose your job or were unable to generate income for some reason. This fund can also been drawn on for unexpected expenses. For instance, Briony used some of it to travel home from university to attend the funeral of a friend who had died suddenly. Liz and Joe emptied their contingency fund when their roof started leaking. In both cases our clients would have had to borrow money, i.e. incur new debt, if they hadn't had their contingency fund.

We suggest that you open a savings account which allows you instant access, so you can draw on it immediately when the need arises. Many of our clients choose an internet savings account. That allows them to transfer the cash needed into their current account without being restricted to bank opening times.

Debt repayments

Your only debt might be a bank overdraft. In that case you simply leave the amount allocated to debt repayment in the account. You might owe money to family and friends, or, most likely, to a variety of creditors. In this case you need to make decisions about how to repay them. We are giving you a number of different options. Whatever you choose to do in the end will need to work in your particular situation. You might actually want to mix and match various approaches.

1. Let's say you are able to include the minimum repayments on your credit card(s) in your cashflow plan. In this case you might want to add the extra money to the amount you pay.

2. You might want to pay the creditor who imposes the highest interest rate first.

3. You might owe money to family or friends. In this case you may feel you should pay them back first.

4. If you have a larger sum available, you may wish to use the percentage approach. To do that you need to know how much you owe to whom, as well as the total amount of debt.

You may have done this exercise already. If not, we recommend that you do it anyway. As you did when you recorded your spending, regard it as a fact-finding mission.

It may take courage. If the final numbers make you gasp or want to hang your head in shame, remember that it is you who are making the judgment on yourself – no-one else. You are neither bad nor mad to have got into this situation. It happened. Take a deep breath and pat yourself on the back for having the guts to finally face up to reality.

We suggest that you now take a break until tomorrow.

When you're ready to carry on, you might have a list like this:

Back taxes	1,500.00
Mortgage Arrears	250.46
Credit Card	781.69
Store Card	432.58
Mum	500.00
TOTAL	**3,464.73**

Treat your total debt of £3,464.73 as 100%. In order to find the percentage for each debt you need to use this formula (to make things easier we are rounding to full numbers):

£		%
Known	-	Unknown
Back taxes		percentage
1,500		????
Known	-	Known
total debt		total percentage
3,465		100%

Formula:

$$\frac{1,500}{3,465} \times 100 = 43.29 \ (43)\%$$

Now repeat this exercise until you have the following list:

Back taxes	1,500.00	43%
Mortgage Arrears	250.46	7%
Credit Card	781.69	23%
Store Card	432.58	13%
Mum	500.00	14%
TOTAL	**3,464.73**	**100%**

Let's say you have £385 available for debt repayment. In order to work out how much you pay each creditor you need this formula (again we are rounding to full numbers):

	£		%
	Known	-	Unknown
Back taxes percentage			amount to repay
	43%		????
	Known	-	Known
	total percentage		total amount
	100%		385

Formula:

43%	-	×
100%	-	385

$$\frac{43}{100} \quad \times \quad 385 \quad = \quad £165.55 \ (166)$$

Again repeat the exercise until your list looks like this:

	Debt	Repayment	
Back taxes	1,500.00	166	43%
Mortgage Arrears	250.46	27	7%
Credit Card	781.69	88	23%
Store Card	432.58	50	13%
Mum	500.00	54	14%
TOTAL	**3,464.73**	**385**	**100%**

No matter which approach you use for your debt repayment, we strongly recommend that you keep a running tally of how much you still owe to whom.

For instance your list could look like this:

Date	Back taxes Re-pay	Back taxes Out-standing	Mortgage Arrears Re-pay	Mortgage Arrears Out-standing	Credit Card Re-pay	Credit Card Out-standing	Store Card Re-pay	Store Card Out-standing	Mum Re-pay	Mum Out-standing
1.9.11		1,500.00		250.46		781.69		432.58		500.00
	10	1,490.00	10	240.46	10	771.69	3	429.58		
16.9.11	166	1,324.00	26	214.46	89	682.69	50	379.58	54	446.00
1.10.11	10	1,314.00	10	204.46	10	672.69				
1.11.11	10	1,304.00	10	194.46	10	662.69				
1.12.11	10	1,294.00	10	184.46	10	652.69				
25.12.11									250	196.00
								Written off		
31.12.11						+49.35	428.93			
						Interest				

Now let's say your mother decided to write off half the money you originally borrowed from her as a Christmas gift. However, the store card company added £49.35 interest to your account at the end of the year.

Now you need to re-calculate your list of outstanding debts accordingly (as of 31st Dec.):

Back taxes	1,294.00	47%
Mortgage Arrears	184.46	7%
Credit Card	652.69	24%
Store Card	428.93	15%
Mum	196.00	7%
TOTAL	**2756.08**	**100%**

Then in January you receive an unexpected windfall of £246. Having divided it by 3, as suggested above, you have another £82 for debt repayment, which you allocate as follows:

	Debt	Repayment	
Back taxes	1,294.00	38	47%
Mortgage Arrears	184.46	5	7%
Credit Card	652.69	20	24%
Store Card	428.93	13	15%
Mum	196.00	6	7%
TOTAL	**2756.08**	**82**	**100%**

Now your debt tally looks like this:

Date	Back taxes Re-pay	Back taxes Out-standing	Mortgage Arrears Re-pay	Mortgage Arrears Out-standing	Credit Card Re-pay	Credit Card Out-standing	Store Card Re-pay	Store Card Out-standing	Mum Re-pay	Mum Out-standing
1.9.11		1,500.00		250.46		781.69		432.58		500.00
	10	1,490.00	10	240.46	10	771.69	3	429.58		
16.9.11	166	1,324.00	26	214.46	89	682.69	50	379.58	54	446.00
1.10.11	10	1,314.00	10	204.46	10	672.69				
1.11.11	10	1,304.00	10	194.46	10	662.69				
1.12.11	10	1,294.00	10	184.46	10	652.69				
25.12.11									250	196.00
								Written off		
31.12.11							+49.35	428.93		
							Interest			
1.1.12	10	1,284.00	10	174.46	10	642.69				
12.1.12	38	1,246.00	5	169.46	20	622.69	13	415.93	6	190.00

Negotiating with creditors

Part of this programme is learning to take responsibility for your financial decisions and being clear about the likely consequences. So if you negotiate a debt-repayment plan don't be tempted to agree to higher repayments than you can **comfortably** accommodate within your cashflow plan.

The cashflow plan will help you to find out how much that is. Eric, for instance, negotiated monthly payments of just £1 with the majority of his creditors. Your creditor(s) will try to talk you into a higher sum by pointing out that, at this rate, you will need decades to repay the debt. However, the clarity your cashflow plan gives you will help you to be much more assertive.

We strongly recommend that if you are finding repaying creditors a headache you seek assistance from an organisation like the UK's Consumer Credit Counselling Service (CCCS) or Citizens' Advice Bureau (CAB). They are much more likely to be able to persuade your creditors to agree a reasonable amount. They will give you a budget. You may wish to follow it, or you may prefer to reach a compromise between your own cashflow plan and their suggestions. But it is important that you stick to the monthly debt repayment amounts they have negotiated for you, and to include those with your Auto Payments (the best method).

If you negotiate debt repayments yourself it is important to understand where both sides are coming from. Your creditor, or debt collection agency, is anxious to recover as much of their debt as possible. Both are motivated by fear; the creditor is afraid to make a loss by having to write off the debt. The debt collection agency, and their staff, are afraid not to earn enough money from the collection. Your motivation is entirely different. It's a desire to live debt-free and prosperously. (If it were otherwise, you wouldn't engage with this programme!) This puts you in a position of strength.

At the same time, it is important to be aware that you are essentially dealing with people. People whose anxieties and worries about money may actually be quite similar to yours. It starts with the person you are dealing with right up to the CEO of the bank or credit card company.

You will find that your creditors vary greatly in their approach. Some debt recovery agencies or departments will pester you on a daily basis, particularly if the amount you owe is large. Other creditors, such as the utility companies, may content themselves for a long time by sending periodic reminders by post. There is a great temptation to follow the principle of the "squeaking wheel gets the most oil" and pay the more demanding creditors first. However, remember that the bank that seems to be taking a relaxed attitude to your debt may suddenly apply for a court order. Conversely, those who constantly pursue you for a debt may quite suddenly accept that you are not going to pay them any faster for all their pleading, and the phone will go quiet. The important point is that YOU are in control of how much you pay and when. Unless there are good reasons to the contrary your plan should make equal provision for all your creditors.

Remember that (in the UK) the credit reference agencies keep detailed records of virtually every loan, credt card or other borrowing from a bank, credit agency or other financial institution. Any late payments you make, or loans on which you default, will appear on your record and may make it difficult or expensive to borrow in the future. So if you think that despite your new approach to money you are going to need new borrowing one day – a mortgage, say, or car finance – you should take great care not to earn any 'black marks'.

Try not to see your creditors as your adversaries, but as people who have the same goal in mind as you do – getting your debt repaid. The only difference is that you're looking at it from different points of view. So be polite but firm. Remember that you can end a telephone call at any time when you feel they are putting too much pressure on you. You can do that politely by saying something like: "I'm sorry, but I can't continue this conversation at this moment. I will call you back tomorrow."

If you do this, make sure you stick to your word by calling back. Equally, make sure that you can keep to whatever sum, and other conditions, you finally agree. That's why it's so important to agree regular debt repayments which you can **comfortably** fit into your cashflow plan.

Once you have agreed a way forward, confirm it in writing. If you are using the phone, ask for the full name of the person you are dealing with and either a postal or email address. Then write something like: "Further to our discussion on the telephone I am writing to confirm that we have agreed ..."

If you send letters, we recommend that you send them by recorded delivery, where the other party has to sign to confirm that they have received the letter and you can check when it has been delivered. In Britain you can do this via the Royal Mail website. It would be prudent to note on your proof of posting when the letter has been delivered and staple it to your copy. Should the creditor take you to court, you have proof of all the negotiations, and the creditor is unable to claim that they haven't received any of your letters.

In some countries it is possible to instruct creditors to contact you only in writing. That makes it much easier to resist any pressure. We think it is much better to negotiate in writing than over the telephone in any case, and it may give you more time. It is helpful to draft a letter or email, leaving it for 24 hours and then reviewing it before sending it off.

If you make an offer of a repayment amount you can then give the creditor a certain amount of time to respond. Two weeks would be reasonable. You could write something like: "If I have not received a reply from you by ... I will assume that you have accepted my offer and will start making payments accordingly." If you can do so, check whether your letter has been delivered. Make a note of the delivery date on the proof of posting you got from the post office.

Then send your cheque with a covering note, saying something like: "I wrote to you on ... Since I have not received a reply from you I assume that my offer of monthly/weekly repayments of £... is acceptable. Therefore I enclose a cheque for

£... to cover the first instalment and I will direct my bank to pay further instalments by standing order." Make sure you then set up the standing order straightaway.

Make sure you keep an orderly record of all your letters and emails. It is important to print them out and keep a hard copy, as well as a log of all phone calls. Remember to follow these with a written confirmation, as described earlier. Should your creditor take you to court you have proof that you have taken appropriate steps to negotiate reasonable repayment terms and that you are committed to repaying the debt.

It is very tempting to agree to higher payments because you want to be debt free as soon as possible. We urge you to resist that temptation. Keeping a debt tally, like the one above, will help you with that. Every month you see the debt go down, especially if you consistently apply the three-way division of every bit of surplus cash and/or windfall money. And you'll be surprised how quickly that will appear in your life.

Lisa and Daniel were paying £10 per month towards their major debt, a loan. They still had over £9,000 of the original £10,000 to pay. They consistently applied the three-way split and their debts were steadily coming down. Then, out of the blue, their major creditor offered to write off the loan if they paid them a lump sum of £2,500 immediately. A benevolent fund linked to their church offered to lend them this money under much better terms than they had had from the commercial lender.

Does that mean that they took on new unsecured debt? No. Before accepting the offer Lisa and Daniel discussed the matter with Sanni. She encouraged them to go ahead, because the original debt had been incurred in the past.

Freeze your credit card – literally!

We suggest that whether or not you are recovering from debt you use a debit card or cheques for any larger purchases, rather than credit cards. For many of our clients, credit cards have become complete no-nos. Others decide to keep one and, literally, freeze it – they quite literally put their one remaining credit card into a water-filled container and store it in the freezer. Why? It means that they do have a credit card for certain purchases they cannot make with either cheque or debit card, or if they want the insurance protection a credit card offers. However, the card needs to be defrosted slowly (any attempt to speed up the process could cause damage to the card). That gives them time to reflect. Do I really need to use the credit card? Do I really need to make the purchase at all? Would it be a good idea to talk to someone before I go ahead?

Yet another example of how debt can be used to serve you – not the other way round.

CHAPTER 4

Cashflow management from day to day

Now let's get back to your cashflow plan. Once you have drawn up the plan you need to monitor what's **actually** happening, with the help of your daily record.

Let's start with your automated payments. We suggest that you deduct them immediately from your bank account, no matter when the cash actually leaves the account. You are committed to paying this money during the course of the month. Therefore we recommend that you regard it as not your money, so you are not tempted to think that you have more money available than you do.

Accordingly, your daily transaction record looks like this:

			Cash	D2D account	Pay account
31.8.11	Balance		4.68	0.00	3.01
1.2	Child Support, Benefit (Aug.)				+320.57
1.1	Salary/Drawings (Aug.)				+1,658.23
1.9.11	Balance				1,981.81
	From Pay a/c	xfer		+1,084.00	-1,084.00
AP	Taxes (current)	DD			-331.60
AP	Mortgage	DD			-125.23
AP	Health Insurance	DD			-35.64
AP	Landline/ISP	DD			-18.58
AP	Mobile/Cell	DD			-35.00
AP	Pension	DD			-74.90
AP	Mortgage Arrears	DD			-10.00
AP	Back Taxes	DD			-10.00
AP	Credit Card	DD			-10.00

On the same day you also transferred the allocated £2 into your contingency fund, and you used the first cheque of the new bank account to send the allocated £3 debt repayment to the store card company.

On your way home from work you went to the ATM and withdrew £50 from the new day-to-day account. You paid cash at the supermarket. Since you have done so well so far you decided to treat yourself and spend your "Frivolity" allowance on a cup of coffee.

Now your daily transaction record looks like this:

			Cash	D2D account	Pay account
31.8.11	Balance		4.68	0.00	3.01
I.2	Child Support, Benefit (Aug.)				+320.57
I.1	Salary/Drawings (Aug.)				+1,658.23
1.9.11	Balance				1,981.81
	From Pay a/c	xfer		+1,084.00	-1,084.00
AP	Taxes (current)	DD			-331.60
AP	Mortgage	DD			-125.23
AP	Health Insurance	DD			-35.64
AP	Landline/ISP	DD			-18.58
AP	Mobile/Cell	DD			-35.00
AP	Pension	DD			-74.90
AP	Mortgage Arrears	DD			-10.00
AP	Back Taxes	DD			-10.00
AP	Credit Card	DD			-10.00
Cont.	Contingency	xfer		-2.00	
DR	Store Card (Debt Repay)	c01		-3.00	
	ATM		+50.00	-50.00	
1.A	Groceries		-14.13		
Friv.	Coffee Shop ("Frivolity")		-1.98		
2.9.11	Balance		38.57	1,029.00	246.86

Did you notice that we said you paid cash for your groceries? That might be a new experience for you. We recommend that from now on you use hard cash (i.e. notes and coins) for all your day-to-day transactions. Why? All our clients tell us that using "real money" helps them to be aware that they are actually spending it. That it feels very different, more real, than using a credit or debit card. It also prevents you from somehow overlooking a payment, which then turns up as a nasty little shock on your statement.

Others say that using cash makes them feel more grounded about money. Shirley had this experience: "I had gone to London for the day. I went into one of the big department stores to make a planned purchase of an electrical item. I used my debit card to pay for it, as I had planned. Then I bought other items, which I usually buy there, but I did not take out cash from the ATM to pay for them. Instead I continued to use the debit card throughout. In the end it almost felt as if I was walking through a fog, as if there was no solid ground under my feet, because I had no idea how much I'd spent. It felt so uncomfortable that I made up my mind to use cash from then on."

Back to our bookkeeping. Let's say that the following day you use your lunch break to open new savings accounts for your special-purpose savings and transfer the allocated sums into them. While you are in the bank you also deposit the refund cheque from the mail order company. Since you planned to include this money with your inflows, you pay it into the "Pay" account. Your bookkeeping looks like this:

			Cash	D2D account	Pay account
31.8.11		Balance	4.68	0.00	3.01
I.2 √		Child Support, Benefit (Aug.)			+320.57
I.1 √		Salary/Drawings (Aug.)			+1,658.23
1.9.11		Balance			1,981.81
		From Pay a/c	xfer	+1,084.00	-1,084.00
AP √		Taxes (current)	DD		-331.60
AP √		Mortgage	DD		-125.23
AP √		Health Insurance	DD		-35.64
AP √		Landline/ISP	DD		-18.58
AP √		Mobile/Cell	DD		-35.00
AP √		Pension	DD		-74.90
AP √		Mortgage Arrears	DD		-10.00
AP √		Back Taxes	DD		-10.00
AP √		Credit Card	DD		-10.00
Cont.		Contingency	xfer	-2.00	
DR		Store Card (Debt Repay)	c01	-3.00	
		ATM	+50.00	-50.00	
1.A		Groceries	-14.13		
Friv.		Coffee Shop ("Frivolity")	-1.98		
2.9.11		Balance	38.57	1,029.00	246.86
SP		Clothing & Accessories	xfer		-50.00
SP		Christmas	xfer		-45.00
SP		Summer Holiday	xfer		-45.00
I.4		Refund (Mail Order Co.)			+33.99
Balance			38.57	1,029.00	140.85

The balance of £140.85 in your payment account roughly tallies with the £134 you allocated for periodic payments (+ the buffer you added to your auto payments and the money that was already in the account). Don't worry if it doesn't tally exactly. The important point is that, over time, a small cushion should build up in this account. Whenever one of the periodic payments is due, for instance when the quarterly gas bill arrives, you should have sufficient money in the "Pay" account to pay the amount out of it.

We recommend that every few days, or at least once a week, you update your cashflow plan to monitor how you are doing against the plan.

Did you notice that we placed ticks next to the regular income items and the Automatic Payment ones? That's because we have already entered them as "spent" in the cashflow plan.

Now you enter the remaining unticked items into the relevant categories in the plan, ticking them off in the transaction record as you go along. As a result your cashflow plan now looks like this:

Sept		Plan	Received	Outstanding
	INFLOWS			
I.1	Salary/Drawings (Aug.)	1,658	1,658.23	0
I.2	Child Support, Benefit (Aug.)	321	320.57	0
I.3	Gifts & Grants			
I.4	Misc.	34	33.99	0
	TOTAL	2,013	2,012.79	
	OUTFLOWS	**Plan**	**Spent/Act**	**Remaining**
AP	Auto Payments	655	655.00	0
PP	Periodic Payments	134	134.00	0
SP	Special Purpose Savings	140	140.00	0
	Sub-Total	929	929.00	
	TOTAL AVAILABLE	1,084	1,083.79	
	Day-to-Day			
1.	**Household**			
1.A	Groceries & Supplies	220	14.13	206
1.B	Children	180		180
1.C	Pets & Garden	36		36
1.D	Eat Out & Take Away Meals	40		40
2.	**Personal Care**			
2.A	Grooming/Make-up	52		52
2.B	Health Care	34		34
2.C	Body Work	45		45
3.	**Transport**			
3.A	Car	80		80
3.B	Public Transport & Taxis	15		15
4.	**Communication**			
4.A	Postage, Stationery, Consumables	38		38
4.B	Reference Books & Mags.	20		20
5.	**Leisure, Friends & Family**			
5.A	Hobbies	60		60
5.B	Entertainment/Fiction	112		112
5.C	Outings	117		117
5.D	Gifts etc.	35		35
	TOTAL	1,084	14.13	
	Surplus	*0*	*1,069.66*	
	Brought forward	*7*	*7.69*	
	TOTAL SURPLUS	*7*	*1,077.35*	
	Frivolity	*2*	*1.98*	*0*
	Contingency	*2*	*2.00*	*0*
	Debt Repayment	*3*	*3.00*	*0*
	TOTAL	*7*	*6.98*	

Your transaction record looks like this:

			Cash	D2D account	Pay account
31.8.11		Balance	4.68	0.00	3.01
I.2	√	Child Support, Benefit (Aug.)			+320.57
I.1	√	Salary/Drawings (Aug.)			+1,658.23
1.9.11		Balance			1,981.81
		From Pay a/c	xfer	+1,084.00	-1,084.00
AP	√	Taxes (current)	DD		-331.60
AP	√	Mortgage	DD		-125.23
AP	√	Health Insurance	DD		-35.64
AP	√	Landline/ISP	DD		-18.58
AP	√	Mobile/Cell	DD		-35.00
AP	√	Pension	DD		-74.90
AP	√	Mortgage Arrears	DD		-10.00
AP	√	Back Taxes	DD		-10.00
AP	√	Credit Card	DD		-10.00
Cont.	√	Contingency	xfer	-2.00	
DR	√	Store Card (Debt Repay)	c01	-3.00	
		ATM	+50.00	-50.00	
1.A	√	Groceries	-14.13		
Friv.	√	Coffee Shop ("Frivolity")	-1.98		
2.9.11		Balance	38.57	1,029.00	246.86
SP	√	Clothing & Accessories	xfer		-60.00
SP	√	Christmas	xfer		-45.00
SP	√	Summer Holiday	xfer		-45.00
I.4	√	Refund (Mail Order Co.)			+33.99
		Balance	38.57	1,029.00	140.85

You might want to add another line at the bottom of your cashflow plan, saying something like "OVERALL SURPLUS". There you deduct the "Total" at the bottom of your surplus categories from the "TOTAL SURPLUS". In our example it looks like this:

Sept		Plan	Received	Outstanding
	INFLOWS			
I.1	Salary/Drawings (Aug.)	1,658	1,658.23	0
I.2	Child Support, Benefit (Aug.)	321	320.57	0
I.3	Gifts & Grants			
I.4	Misc.	34	33.99	0
	TOTAL	2,013	2,012.79	
	OUTFLOWS	**Plan**	**Spent/Act**	**Remaining**
AP	Auto Payments	655	655.00	0
PP	Periodic Payments	134	134.00	0
SP	Special Purpose Savings	140	140.00	0
	Sub-Total	929	929.00	
	TOTAL AVAILABLE	1,084	1,083.79	
	Day-to-Day			
1.	**Household**			
1.A	Groceries & Supplies	220	14.13	206
1.B	Children	180		180
1.C	Pets & Garden	36		36
1.D	Eat Out & Take Away Meals	40		40
2.	**Personal Care**			
2.A	Grooming/Make-up	52		52
2.B	Health Care	34		34
2.C	Body Work	45		45
3.	**Transport**			
3.A	Car	80		80
3.B	Public Transport & Taxis	15		15
4.	**Communication**			
4.A	Postage, Stationery, Consumables	38		38
4.B	Reference Books & Mags.	20		20
5.	**Leisure, Friends & Family**			
5.A	Hobbies	60		60
5.B	Entertainment/Fiction	112		112
5.C	Outings	117		117
5.D	Gifts etc.	35		35
	TOTAL	1,084	14.13	
	Surplus	0	1,069.66	
	Brought forward	7	7.69	
	TOTAL SURPLUS	7	1,077.35	
	Frivolity	2	1.98	0
	Contingency	2	2.00	0
	Debt Repayment	3	3.00	0
	TOTAL	7	6.98	
	OVERALL SURPLUS	0	1,070	

If you add together the cash you have in your purse (£38.57) and the £1,029.00 left in your "D2D account" you will get £1,067.57. If you round that up to £1,068 you are within £2 of the "OVERALL SURPLUS" in the "Spent/Act(ual)" column. That gives you a check to see that what is happening in your pocket and bank account tallies with your cashflow plan. It doesn't have to match exactly. If the two sums are within £2-3 of each other you are pretty much on the right track.

Make sure that the formula in the last column swaps depending on whether you are working with inflows or outflows. In order to find out if and how much of the money you expect to come in is outstanding, you need to deduct what you expect in the "Plan" column from what you have actually received in the second column. On the outflow side you need to deduct what you have actually spent to date from the amount you are planning to spend to find out how much you have left in that category.

If you use a spreadsheet your formulae look like this:

	A	B	C	D	E
1	Sept		Plan	Received	Outstanding
2		**INFLOWS**			
3	I.1	Salary/Drawings (Aug.)			=D3-C3
4	I.2	Child Support, Benefit (Aug.)			=D4-C4
5	I.3	Gifts & Grants			=D5-C5
6	I.4	Misc.			=D6-C6
7		TOTAL	=SUM(C3:C6)	=SUM(D3:D6)	
8		**OUTFLOWS**	**Plan**	**Spent/Act**	**Remaining**
9	AP	Auto Payments			=C9-D9
10	PP	Periodic Payments			=C10-D10
11	SP	Special Purpose Savings			=C11-D11
12		Sub-Total	=SUM(C9:C11)	=SUM(D9:D11)	
13		**TOTAL AVAILABLE**	=C7-C12	=D7-D12	
14		**Day-to-Day**			
15	**1.**	**Household**			
16	1.A	Groceries & Supplies			=C16-D16
17	1.B	Children			=C17-D17
18	1.C	Pets & Garden			=C18-D18
19	1.D	Eat Out & Take Away Meals			=C19-D19
20	**2.**	**Personal Care**			
21	2.A	Grooming/Make-up			=C21-D21
22	2.B	Health Care			=C22-D22
23	2.C	Body Work			=C23-D23
24	**3.**	**Transport**			
25	3.A	Car			=C25-D25
26	3.B	Public Transport & Taxis			=C26-D26
27	**4.**	**Communication**			
28	4.A	Postage, Stationery, Consumables			=C28-D28
29	4.B	Reference Books & Mags.			=C29-D29
30	**5.**	**Leisure, Friends & Family**			
31	5.A	Hobbies			=C31-D31
32	5.B	Entertainment/Fiction			=C32-D32
33	5.C	Outings			=C33-D33
34	5.D	Gifts etc.			=C34-D34
35		TOTAL	=SUM(C16:C34)	=Sum(D16:D34)	
36		*Surplus*	=C13-C35	=D13-D35	
37		*Brought forward*			
38		***TOTAL SURPLUS***	=SUM(C36:C37)	=Sum(D36:D37)	
39		*Frivolity*			=C39-D39
40		*Contingency*			=C40-D40
41		*Debt Repayment*			=C41-D41
42		*TOTAL*	=SUM(C39:C41)	=Sum(D39:D41)	
43		**OVERALL SURPLUS**	=C38-C42	=D38-D42	

Some spreadsheet users will place the "OVERALL SURPLUS" row at the very top and then freeze the panes. That way they can always see how much money is still available, no matter where they have scrolled to.

What about the "Pay" account? If you decide to use a separate current account for your day-to-day expenditure you can ignore what is going on there for cash-flow planning purposes. However, in order to stay aware of how much money you have where and for what, you do need to keep a check on your transactions and balances in all your accounts to make sure they correspond with your own records. This is called "bank reconciliation" or, if you live in the U.S. "balancing your checkbook".

We recommend that you sign up to internet banking and do it weekly. Alternatively you could get a slip with your recent transactions from the ATM. If you reconcile weekly there are only a few transactions to tally, so it shouldn't take more than about 10 minutes. On the other hand, if you're confronted with two sheets of transactions for a month, you may well be tempted not to do the reconciliation at all because it's such a big job. And you are back in vagueness. Remember that it is often vagueness and a sense that you may not have enough money that get you into trouble and make you feel stressed.

How do you do your bank reconciliation? Let's say you get the online statement for your "D2D account" and it says £1,032.00, but your books say £1,029.00. You go through all the transactions in your account and place a tick against those that have been recorded by the bank, both on your record and on the statement. Accordingly, your transaction record now looks like this:

			Cash	D2D account	Pay account
31.8.11		Balance	4.68	0.00	3.01
I.2	√	Child Support, Benefit (Aug.)			+320.57
I.1	√	Salary/Drawings (Aug.)			+1,658.23
1.9.11		Balance			1,981.81
		From Pay a/c	xfer	√+1,084.00	-1,084.00
AP	√	Taxes (current)	DD		-331.60
AP	√	Mortgage	DD		-125.23
AP	√	Health Insurance	DD		-35.64
AP	√	Landline/ISP	DD		-18.58
AP	√	Mobile/Cell	DD		-35.00
AP	√	Pension	DD		-74.90
AP	√	Mortgage Arrears	DD		-10.00
AP	√	Back Taxes	DD		-10.00
AP	√	Credit Card	DD		-10.00
Cont.	√	Contingency	xfer	√-2.00	
DR	√	Store Card (Debt Repay)	c01	-3.00	
		ATM	+50.00	√-50.00	
1.A	√	Groceries		-14.13	
Friv.	√	Coffee Shop ("Frivolity")		-1.98	
2.9.11		Balance	38.57	1,029.00	246.86
SP	√	Clothing & Accessories	xfer		-50.00
SP	√	Christmas	xfer		-45.00
SP	√	Summer Holiday	xfer		-45.00
I.4	√	Refund (Mail Order Co.)			+33.99
		Balance	38.57	√1,029.00	140.85

Now you take your book balance of £1,029 and add to it all the transactions which have not yet been recorded by the bank. In our case it's £3 (the cheque for the Store Card Debt Repayment). That gives you a sum of £1,032 – the same as your bank statement. This means that the two records tally, i.e. reconcile.

Less often, you may have paid or transferred money into your account which does not yet show on the bank statement. In that case you deduct the amount from the balance in your transaction record so that the two tally. Once they reconcile, we recommend that you tick both the balance in your books and the bank balance to tell you that they tally, and then keep your printout until the next reconciliation.

If the two records don't reconcile, it's most likely that you have made a mistake and you need to go back through your transactions to look for it. Sometimes it's simply an adding-up error. At other times you may have recorded the amount wrongly in your books. In these days of computerised accounting by the banks it's more likely that the error is with you, but that does not mean that they don't make mistakes. If you do your bank reconciliation weekly, you are more likely to find any errors quickly.

If you have ticked the last balance in your book as correct you also know how far back you need to go to find the mistake. If you simply cannot find it there and then we suggest that you leave it, sleep it over and go back to it the next day. But do go back – it's very likely that you'll find what's wrong then. As a last resort you could always go to the bank and ask for assistance. Don't give in to the temptation to just leave it altogether. You may feel very stressed in the short-term, but that will only last until you have sorted out the discrepancy. If you leave it altogether you are in danger of getting back into vagueness, stress and worrying that you don't have enough money.

To help you with the bank reconciliation, we recommend that you use a different colour for your ticks so that they stand out. That way you can more easily identify the transactions which have not yet been recorded by the bank. In our example we have used a colour coding for our bookkeeping: blue for money going in and red for money going out. Some people may prefer simply to put "+" or "-" in front of the number. Remember that whichever method you choose must work for you and, of course, that you can change at any time.

Now let's look at reconciling your "Pay account". For the sake of this exercise we assume that you received your child support payment on 3rd September. It will not be included in the cashflow plan until you draw up the one for October. Now you have two choices, depending on which you find easier to manage. Some people decide to leave the inflowing money out of their transaction record until the end of the month, when they enter it together with their main income in both their daily transaction record and the cashflow plan for October. They just make a note on the printout of the online statement saying something like "Child support 320.57 (3.9.)".

Let's look at how your transaction record will look in this case:

			Cash	D2D account	Pay account
31.8.11		Balance	4.68	0.00	3.01
I.2	√	Child Support, Benefit (Aug.)			√ +320.57
I.1	√	Salary/Drawings (Aug.)			√+1,658.23
1.9.11		Balance			1,981.81
		From Pay a/c	xfer	√+1,084.00	√-1,084.00
AP	√	Taxes (current)	DD		-331.60
AP	√	Mortgage	DD		√-125.23
AP	√	Health Insurance	DD		-35.64
AP	√	Landline/ISP	DD		-18.58
AP	√	Mobile/Cell	DD		-35.00
AP	√	Pension	DD		√-74.90
AP	√	Mortgage Arrears	DD		√-10.00
AP	√	Back Taxes	DD		√-10.00
AP	√	Credit Card	DD		√-10.00
Cont.	√	Contingency	xfer	√-2.00	
DR	√	Store Card (Debt Repay)	c01	-3.00	
		ATM	+50.00	√-50.00	
1.A	√	Groceries	-14.13		
Friv.	√	Coffee Shop ("Frivolity")	-1.98		
2.9.11		Balance	38.57	1,029.00	246.86
SP	√	Clothing & Accessories	xfer		√-50.00
SP	√	Christmas	xfer		√-45.00
SP	√	Summer Holiday	xfer		√-45.00
I.4	√	Refund (Mail Order Co.)			√+33.99
		Balance	38.57	√1,029.00	140.85

Note: Child support 320.57 (3.9.)

We assume that some of your auto payments have not yet been deducted from your account, and your bank balance shows £882.24. As you did for your "D2D account" you need to add these to your book balance of £140.85, i.e.:

```
 140.85
+331.60
+ 35.64
+ 18.58
+ 35.00
 561.67
```

Now you need to add the child benefit payment you have received; i.e.:

```
561.67
+320.57
882.24
```

Other people will enter money coming in in the daily transaction record, but not include it into their cashflow plan until they draw up the October plan. Accordingly their daily book looks like this:

			Cash	D2D account	Pay account
31.8.11		Balance	4.68	0.00	3.01
I.2 √		Child Support, Benefit (Aug.)			√ +320.57
I.1 √		Salary/Drawings (Aug.)			√+1,658.23
1.9.11		Balance			1,981.81
		From Pay a/c	xfer	√+1,084.00	√-1,084.00
AP √		Taxes (current)	DD		-331.60
AP √		Mortgage	DD		√-125.23
AP √		Health Insurance	DD		-35.64
AP √		Landline/ISP	DD		-18.58
AP √		Mobile/Cell	DD		-35.00
AP √		Pension	DD		√-74.90
AP √		Mortgage Arrears	DD		√-10.00
AP √		Back Taxes	DD		√-10.00
AP √		Credit Card	DD		√-10.00
Cont. √		Contingency	xfer	√-2.00	
DR √		Store Card (Debt Repay)	c01	-3.00	
		ATM	+50.00	√-50.00	
1.A √		Groceries	-14.13		
Friv. √		Coffee Shop ("Frivolity")	-1.98		
2.9.11		Balance	38.57	1,029.00	246.86
SP √		Clothing & Accessories	xfer		√-50.00
SP √		Christmas	xfer		√-45.00
SP √		Summer Holiday	xfer		√-45.00
I.4 √		Refund (Mail Order Co.)			√+33.99
3.9.11		Balance	38.57	√1,029.00	140.85
I.2		Child Support, Benefit (for Oct.)			√+320.57
		Balance	38.57	1,029.00	461.42

And the bank reconciliation looks like this: 461.42
+331.60
+ 35.64
+ 18.58
+ 35.00
882.24

We also suggest that you physically count the cash in your pocket every time you update your transaction record. Cash is notorious for not agreeing with what your books say you are supposed to have. You may have been given the wrong change in a shop, not been given a receipt, or perhaps you put a few coins into a collection tin and forgot about it.

So what do you do if the cash in your pocket does not tally with your transaction record? Let's say you have been given too much change in a shop. Then you simply add it under your "Misc" inflow category in the "Received" column. It could look like this:

Sept		Plan	Received	Outstanding
	INFLOWS			
I.1	Salary/Drawings (Aug.)	1,658	1,658.23	0
I.2	Child Support, Benefit (Aug.)	321	320.57	0
I.3	Gifts & Grants			
I.4	Misc	34	34.99	+1
	TOTAL	2,013	2,013.79	

If instead you're missing some cash, the more likely scenario, you could add another category. Some of our clients argue that this is a donation they have made to some unknown person and include it in there, or you could add a "Misc" category on your outflow side and record it there. That way both your transaction record and your cashflow plan correspond with each other.

This brings us to the topic of charitable giving. Some of our clients feel strongly that they should give a regular donation to their church or other charity, perhaps a 10% tithe. For us the important point is how it fits in with your own needs and circumstances. If you tithe 10% but end up feeling deprived, you will feel worse, not better. Yet not tithing will make you feel guilty. It's up to you to find the compromise that is most satisfactory for you. Perhaps you could give 10% of any surplus and windfalls before doing the three-way split between "Frivolity", "Contingency" and "Debt Repayment" – many of our clients adopt this method. This formula also makes the arithmetic easier because once you have deducted the 10% the remainder is always divisible by 3. For instance, say you have been given £250. Dividing it by 3 will give you £83.33. but if you deduct 10% (£25) you are left with £225, which, divided by 3, makes £75.

Giving out of our largesse to those less fortunate than we are increases our sense of prosperity. Even if it's only a small amount, it still gives us the sense that we have enough money to give away.

You are already in the habit of keeping a daily record of your spending from the tracking exercise you did earlier. We strongly recommend that you continue this habit and that you update your cashflow plan at least once a week. It's important that you maintain both records simultaneously. The daily transaction record gives you the data you need so that your cashflow plan gives you meaningful information. That way you are always on top of your finances: You know how much money you have where and for what.

We have developed software to help you do this more easily and quickly, designed to complement this guide. The software is available from our website at **www.holisticmoneymanager.com/software** You can also buy it as a smartphone app.

It is very likely that in the course of the month you end up spending more than planned in one category. This tends to happen from the second week onwards. Being up to date with all your numbers will give you a choice about how to deal with it.

Let's say you have just updated your cashflow plan and it looks like this:

Sept		Plan	Received	Outstanding
	INFLOWS			
I.1	Salary/Drawings (Aug.)	1,658	1,658.23	0
I.2	Child Support, Benefit (Aug.)	321	320.57	0
I.3	Gifts & Grants			
I.4	Misc.	34	33.99	0
	TOTAL	2,013	2,012.79	
	OUTFLOWS	**Plan**	**Spent/Act**	**Remaining**
AP	Auto Payments	655	655.00	0
PP	Periodic Payments	134	134.00	0
SP	Special Purpose Savings	140	140.00	0
	Sub-Total	929	929.00	
	TOTAL AVAILABLE	1,084	1,083.79	
	Day-to-Day			
1.	**Household**			
1.A	Groceries & Supplies	220	184.37	36
1.B	Children	180	142.50	38
1.C	Pets & Garden	36	21.12	15
1.D	Eat Out & Take Away Meals	40	48.00	-8
2.	**Personal Care**			
2.A	Grooming/Make-up	52	33.58	18
2.B	Health Care	34	12.32	22
2.C	Body Work	45	30.00	15
3.	**Transport**			
3.A	Car	80	44.15	36
3.B	Public Transport & Taxis	15		15
4.	**Communication**			
4.A	Postage, Stationery, Consumables	38	44.31	-6
4.B	Reference Books & Mags.	20	7.85	12
5.	**Leisure, Friends & Family**			
5.A	Hobbies	60	48.75	11
5.B	Entertainment/Fiction	112	98.45	14
5.C	Outings	117	117.00	0
5.D	Gifts etc.	35	16.99	18
	TOTAL	**1,084**	**849.39**	
	Surplus	*0*	*234.40*	
	Brought forward	*7*	*7.69*	
	TOTAL SURPLUS	*7*	*242.09*	
	Frivolity	*2*	*1.98*	0
	Contingency	*2*	*2.00*	0
	Debt Repayment	*3*	*3.00*	0
	TOTAL	*7*	*6.98*	
	OVERALL SURPLUS	**0**	**235**	

You have spent more money than planned in two categories. Before we look at the choices you have, we want to stress that there is nothing wrong with that. Joe initially had lots of problems with updating his cashflow plan and looking at the figures in the last column. He called it "facing up to what went right and what went wrong." That is **NOT** the purpose of this exercise! We cannot stress that too much.

The last column enables you to do what accountants call "variance analysis". The important word here is "analysis", which asks the question "why"? So why did you spend more than planned on eating out? The answer might be simply that you went to your favourite restaurant and they'd put up their prices. Or when you drew up your cashflow plan you forgot that you needed to buy a new cartridge for your printer. Should you have turned around at the restaurant when you realised their prices had gone up to stay within your planned expenditure? Absolutely not! Should you have hung in there, hoping that your print cartridge would last until the end of the month, getting stressed and anxious every time you printed a document? Nope!

If you now go through the plan you will find that you have room to manoeuvre. At this point in the month you'll probably have a pretty good idea how much more you are likely to spend on the various categories. Let's say that you spot straightaway that you won't spend more than another £30 on your car before the end of the month. That gives you immediately the £6 you need to move into the "Postage, Stationery, Consumables" category. To make up the £8 overspend "Eat Out & Take Away Meals" category you decide to take £2 from "Health Care", £3 from "Hobbies", and another £3 from "Groceries & Supplies".

Accordingly your cashflow plan now looks like this:

Sept		Plan	Received	Outstanding
	INFLOWS			
I.1	Salary/Drawings (Aug.)	1,658	1,658.23	0
I.2	Child Support, Benefit (Aug.)	321	320.57	0
I.3	Gifts & Grants			
I.4	Misc	34	33.99	0
	TOTAL	2,013	2,012.79	
	OUTFLOWS	**Plan**	**Spent/Act**	**Remaining**
AP	Auto Payments	655	655.00	0
PP	Periodic Payments	134	134.00	0
SP	Special Purpose Savings	140	140.00	0
	Sub-Total	929	929.00	
	TOTAL AVAILABLE	1,084	1,083.79	
	Day-to-Day			
1.	**Household**			
1.A	Groceries & Supplies	217	184.37	33
1.B	Children	180	142.50	38
1.C	Pets & Garden	36	21.12	15
1.D	Eat Out & Take Away Meals	48	48.00	0
2.	**Personal Care**			
2.A	Grooming/Make-up	52	33.58	18
2.B	Health Care	32	12.32	20
2.C	Body Work	45	30.00	15
3.	**Transport**			
3.A	Car	74	44.15	30
3.B	Public Transport & Taxis	15		15
4.	**Communication**			
4.A	Postage, Stationery, Consumables	44	44.31	0
4.B	Reference Books & Mags.	20	7.85	12
5.	**Leisure, Friends & Family**			
5.A	Hobbies	57	48.75	8
5.B	Entertainment/Fiction	112	98.45	14
5.C	Outings	117	117.00	0
5.D	Gifts etc.	35	16.99	18
	TOTAL	**1,084**	**849.39**	
	Surplus	*0*	*234.40*	
	Brought forward	*7*	*7.69*	
	TOTAL SURPLUS	**7**	**242.09**	
	Frivolity	*2*	*1.98*	*0*
	Contingency	*2*	*2.00*	*0*
	Debt Repayment	*3*	*3.00*	*0*
	TOTAL	**7**	**6.98**	
	OVERALL SURPLUS	**0**	**235**	

If you diligently continue keeping your books and monitoring what's going on, you will find that you need to adjust your cashflow plan more than once during the month. That is its purpose! The plan gives you clarity about your financial situation. This clarity gives you choices. Having choices gives you a sense of prosperity.

CHAPTER 5

Surviving the money jungle

In this chapter we look at some additional ways of staying smart around money.

Paying Taxes

What about putting money aside for taxes? In our example we assume that your income tax is deducted at source by your employer, or that you are exempt from paying because your income is too low. The tax we have included in the cashflow plan is a local tax (Council Tax in the UK) which is paid via Auto Payment. If you're self-employed we recommend that you read Sanni's book for sole traders which deals with the issue in detail.

But what if you have additional income? Or if you're retired and have to pay some income tax, which is not deducted at source? Your accountant will tell you which proportion of income you need to set aside to make any lump sum payments to the tax authorities when they become due.

We strongly recommend that you make it as difficult as possible for yourself to access this money. That will reduce the temptation to spend it "when things get a bit tight". A postal account with a notice period is ideal. Keeping orderly books will enable you to submit your tax return as early as possible. Therefore you will know well in advance when you are due to pay your taxes and how much. Then you mark in your diary or calendar the date you need to give notice to withdraw those funds.

What if your records show that you have saved too much for taxes? That's a situation we'd all like to be in. We suggest you withdraw all the money you have saved, pay the tax and treat the remainder as a windfall. If you have not saved enough, you may need to use money from your contingency fund to make up the shortfall. It is worth doing that, because owing taxes causes a lot of stress and pressure. At the same time you may need to sit down, possibly with your accountant, and figure out why you have set aside too little, so that it won't happen again.

Managing money as a couple or family

In our experience one partner usually assumes responsibility for the family finances. Most couples and families find that they keep three cashflow plans with three corresponding sets of books: one for each partner and one for the household. Accordingly each partner and the household have their own bank accounts. The household account(s) could be joint account(s) or set up so that only one partner has access. It all depends on your particular circumstances.

In some instances one partner will pay the other a contribution towards the household expenditure, who then includes this in their own cashflow planning. There are numerous variations on this theme. As with everything else, you need to work out whichever works best for your particular circumstances.

Below is George's cashflow plan. His Auto Payments are for personal pension and insurance payments. He pays £750 into the joint account each month and saves £50 towards "Holiday & Weekend Breaks", £40 for "Gifts" and £25 for "Clothing". Geraldine, his partner, does most of the household shopping, but he allows £20 for the odd items he picks up. He allows £55 to allow him to treat the two of them to a meal. He spends about £20 a month on his hobbies and £25 on entertainment.

Mar		Plan	Received	Outstanding
	INFLOWS			
I.1	Salary (Feb.)	1,320	1,320.12	0
I.2	Gifts & Grants			0
I.3	Misc			
	TOTAL	1,320	1,320.12	
	OUTFLOWS	**Plan**	**Spent/Act**	**Remaining**
AP	Auto Payments	305	305.00	0
JA	Joint Account	750	750.00	0
SP	Special Purpose Savings	115	115.00	0
	Sub-Total	1,170	1,170.00	
	TOTAL AVAILABLE	150	150.12	
	Day-to-Day			
1.	**Household**			
1.A	Groceries & Supplies	20		20
1.B	Eat Out & Take Away Meals	55		55
2.	**Personal Care**			
2.A	Grooming	7		7
2.B	Health Care			
3.	**Leisure, Friends & Family**			
3.A	Hobbies	20		20
3.B	Entertainment	25		25
	TOTAL	127		
	Surplus	23		
	Brought forward	15	15.86	
	TOTAL SURPLUS	**38**	15.86	
	Frivolity	12		0
	Contingency	12		0
	Debt Repayment	12		0
	TOTAL	**36**		
	OVERALL SURPLUS	**2**		

We do strongly recommend that you talk regularly about money, at least once a month before drawing up the cashflow plan. Make a date with each other and meet formally, preferably at a table, at the appointed time. We also recommend that you include any children who are old enough to participate.

Some families find it helpful to light a candle. For as long as the candle is burning every person has the right to speak without interruption. The other person(s) try to really listen without preparing their response/counter argument in their head. That can be quite difficult. Others use a significant object, such as a "speaking stone". It is placed on the table and the person who takes the object has the right to speak for as long as they hold the object.

We also suggest that you start the meeting punctually, as you would a business meeting, and that you allocate a definite amount of time. Depending on the frequency of your meetings this could be anywhere between one and two hours. All these methods are designed to help take out any emotional heat from the debate and keep it objective.

Travelling abroad and foreign currency

How do you manage your money when you travel in a foreign country with a different currency? Let's assume you've paid for your travel and accommodation in advance. If you expect to pay your hotel bill at the end of your stay, we suggest you ring-fence that money. One way to do that would be to transfer the necessary funds into your "Pay Account" and pay with something like a VISA debit card, which can be used just like a credit card, both for hotel reservations and hire cars.

Many consumer organisations advise the use of a credit card for purchases abroad. In the case of a dispute over the goods or services, the card company is jointly liable for purchases above a certain amount and you can claim your money back from them. You really need to think carefully about that.

Of course, if credit card use has got you into trouble in the past your financial recovery, clarity and prosperity may well be worth far more than any sense of security a credit card might give you. If you can trust yourself to keep accurate records of all your spending on the card and not "go off the rails" with it, it might be the more appropriate method. Whatever you decide, you may need to shop around to find a card provider who does not charge for foreign transactions.

We most strongly suggest that you do not charge any incidental spending in the hotel to your room. That way you can only too easily lose your clarity. We recommend you use cash or travellers' cheques instead. Some people take all their spending money in cash and use a money belt to keep it safe. Others allocate a certain sum in the foreign currency and use a debit card to withdraw it from a local ATM. Again you need to decide for yourself what will work best for you.

We suggest that you create a spending plan, similar to your monthly cashflow plan, for your trip, and that you keep track of your spending in the same way. Below is an example of a one-week self-catering holiday abroad, all figures are in the foreign currency. It assumes that all travel to the destination and accommodation have been paid in advance.

		Plan	Received	Outstanding
	TOTAL AVAILABLE	550	550.00	
		Plan	Spent/Act	Remaining
1.	**Household**			
1.A	Groceries & Supplies	75		
1.B	Eat Out & Take Away Meals	125		
2.	**Personal Care**			
2.A	Grooming	25		
2.B	Health Care	25		
3.	**Transport**			
3.A	Bike Hire	84		
3.B	Public Transport	50		
4.	**Leisure, Friends & Family**			
3.A	Entertainment & Attractions	115		
3.B	Souvenirs & Gifts	35		
3.C	Postcards & Stamps	15		
	TOTAL	**549**		
	SURPLUS	**1**		

Remember to update your day-to-day transaction record in your own currency every time you withdraw cash from an ATM abroad. You won't be able to deduct the exact amount until you have looked at your bank statement. Some people use the rate they received at their last exchange and then correct the amount when they have checked their statement. Others simply keep the ATM receipt as a reminder.

Juggling with weeks and months

What do you do if you're paid weekly but some of your outgoings are calculated per calendar month – or vice versa? The temptation here is to multiply the weekly amount by 52 and then divide by 12, or multiply the monthly amount by 12 and divide by 52. Over time you will end up with a deficit because the year has more than exactly 52 weeks (52 weeks and 1 day, to be precise). Therefore we recommend working out the daily rate and then adjusting.

Let's say your income is paid weekly but your rent/mortgage is deducted per calendar month. First you need to work out how much your rent is per annum. Let's say the monthly amount is £413.92. You multiply that by 12, which is £4,967.04. You then divide this amount by the number of days in a year, i.e. 365. You then get a daily amount of £13.61 You then multiply that by the number of days in a week, i.e. 7 which gives you £95.26. This is the amount you need to put aside each week for your rent.

The formula is: weekly amount = monthly amount x 12 / 365 x 7

What if the situation is the other way round, i.e. you are paid per calendar month, but your rent is calculated weekly? Let's say the weekly amount is £95.26. You divide this by 7, which gives you a daily rate of £13.61. You then multiply that by 365 to get the annual figure, which is £4,967.13 Lastly you divide that by 12 to give you the monthly amount of £413.93.

The formula is: monthly amount = weekly amount / 7 x 365 / 12

(If you were to use the simple formula of multiplying the weekly rent by 52 and then dividing by 12 you would pay £412.79 per month. That makes a difference of £1.14 per month. By the end of the year you would have underpaid £13.68. Whenever you move out your landlord is likely to demand that amount and you could be left with a hefty back payment.)

In Britain social security benefits are calculated on a weekly basis and paid either fortnightly or every 4 weeks. If it's every 4 weeks you actually receive 13 payments in a year, i.e. there is one month when you receive one payment at the beginning of the month and another at the end.

If you work on a monthly cashflow plan we recommend that you include the normal payments you receive with your monthly income, and the one extra payment as a windfall.

What do you do if you have different income periods? For instance, Ken, who has mental health issues and mild learning difficulties, receives one type of benefit payment every fortnight and another every 4 weeks. He pays rent weekly, but his other bills are calculated per calendar month. Ken has only one current account and lived in constant fear of overdrawing and then incurring high charges which he would not be able to repay easily, thus getting into debt. Therefore he wanted to build up a buffer to prevent this happening.

We used the formula above to work out Ken's weekly inflows and the money he needs to put aside for his rent and bills (rounded up to build up the buffer). From his spending records we worked out how much he needs for his day-to-day spending and how much is appropriate to save for occasional treats, day trips and for Christmas.

He now withdraws a certain amount of cash each fortnight when his main benefit has been paid. From this he puts the agreed amounts for treats, day trips and Christmas into old-fashioned money boxes. He then divides the remaining cash into one envelope for each of his day-to-day spending categories. This system works well for him. He actually enjoys "juggling" the cash between the different envelopes.

Using your contingency fund

If you need to make an urgent unexpected purchase, the money may need to come out of your contingency fund. After all, that's what it's there for. However, you may find yourself reluctant to use it. That reluctance is often based on fear that something else will happen and that you will run out of money. To counteract that fear, it's helpful to tell yourself how well off you are to have this money available and to "pat yourself on the back" for having this prudent reserve. It also helps to tell yourself that you will rebuild your contingency fund faster than you did the first time round because your overall financial situation is so much better.

We recommend that you get three offers or quotes for your purchase, preferably in writing. Then you compare those quotes and make a decision based on your needs rather than on price alone. Which is the most appropriate for your needs? It might actually be the most expensive of the three, perhaps because you have reason to believe the product will last longer or cost less to maintain – the longest-lasting car tyres, for example, are unlikely to be the cheapest. You have to ask yourself honestly, though, if you want to go with this one for the prestige or because it is the best for your particular circumstances.

Once you have decided which is the most suitable the next question will be if you have the money for it. Your books should tell you if you have enough money in another fund that you could draw on, should there not be enough in the contingency fund to cover the expenditure. This is preferable to incurring debt. Remember how stressed you were when you had debts. Remember also that you always pay a higher interest rate for borrowed money than you earn on savings.

You can avoid having to dip into your contingency fund by anticipating some expenses. In the final chapter we will describe the "prosperity formula" where we recommend that you save 40% of your available funds in various ways, with the last 10% going to charity. We will also give you some other suggestions. You may want to adapt them according to your personal circumstances.

For instance in your "special purpose savings" you may want to build up a fund for home maintenance. Then you can use the money in this fund to redecorate or replace soft furnishings, furniture and appliances as soon as they show signs of ageing. That way you can make a considered choice rather than having to make a quick decision because something broke. If you live a long way from your family, you might also want to have a travel fund both for planned and emergency family visits. And if you are a home-owner you might want to designate the "long-term capital savings/investments" fund for investment into your property.

Entering into contracts with suppliers

We recommend that whenever you enter into a long-term contract with a supplier, e.g. a utility company, you also get three quotes. Once you have decided which one is your preferred supplier we strongly recommend that you read carefully through their Terms & Conditions, preferably the day before you sign up. That will give you time to reflect on them overnight.

Herbert wanted a certain service which came as part of a package. The salesperson had left him with the impression that he needed to buy the whole package, but when he read through the Terms & Conditions he discovered that he did not need to do that. He called the company and changed his order. He now pays about half of the originally quoted price.

Sanni says that when she set up the Holistic Money Manager website, she made an appointment with the representative of a company which was to supply her telephone and internet service. The night before, she read through the Terms & Conditions where it said something like: "... use for commercial purposes is prohibited." As a consequence she cancelled the appointment, because she wanted the service for commercial purposes. The representative assured her that those Terms & Conditions were out of date and that the company "just hadn't got round to changing them yet". Having read through them gave Sanni the assertiveness to quietly say that she was not prepared to proceed under these circumstances, because she would be in the wrong should there ever be a dispute with the company.

Handling disputes

When you have a dispute with a supplier you proceed in a similar way as you did when negotiating with creditors. However, if you feel emotionally too involved, especially when you are really angry, it might be better to contact the company in writing. It's also a good idea to wait 24 hours after having drafted a letter or email and review it when you are calmer before sending it off.

Sylvia was furious when, despite numerous calls to her ISP's customer service department, they failed to reconnect her internet following some technical changes they had made. She made one final, very angry, call telling them that she had "had enough of them". She then switched to another ISP. Since Sylvia needed the internet for her work she wrote to her old ISP claiming breach of contract and compensation for loss of earnings. The case eventually went to the ombudsman service where the company stated that she had cancelled her contract with the comment in that last phone call and that therefore they were not liable.

If you are using the phone, ask for the full name of the person you are dealing with and either a postal or email address. Then once you have agreed how and how soon the company is going to put things right, confirm it in writing. Write something like: "Further to our discussion on the telephone I am writing to confirm that we have agreed ..."

We recommend that you send letters by recorded delivery, so the other party has to sign to confirm that they have received the letter and you can check when it has been delivered. In Britain you can do this via the Royal Mail website. It would be prudent to note on your proof of posting when the letter has been delivered and staple it to your copy.

Make sure you keep an orderly record of all your letters and emails. It might be helpful to print them out and keep a hard copy, as well as a log of all phone calls. Remember to follow calls with a written confirmation, as described above. Should you want to take the case to the ombudsman service or to court, you have proof that you have given the company reasonable time to put things right.

Impulse shopping

It can be very hard to resist buying on impulse, especially when it appears to be a bargain. Remember that retailers earn a living by selling and that they are likely to resort to any number of methods to entice you to buy. You go in to a shop just to buy a few groceries and spot an item you suddenly feel you absolutely need, and that at the price it's an incredible bargain.

How do you resist the temptation? One way is to adopt the "72 hour rule". This is a tool used by Debtors Anonymous. We think it is a useful device anybody could benefit from, not just compulsive shoppers. The "72 hour rule" means that you leave 72 hours between spotting the "bargain" and buying it. Some people don't take that long, but most will leave at least 24 hours. Use the time to talk through with someone whether this would be a prudent purchase. The rule is especially important on low-value items. It is so easy to fritter money away on these little things that only cost a few pennies. They soon mount up.

Another way is to use a shopping list. It might be a good idea to carry a little note-book with you at all times. Whenever you run low on something you regularly use, or something you are lacking, write it on your list. If you spot a bargain, especially of an item you buy regularly, see if you can find out for how long the special offer will last. Then, after your time of reflection, add the item to the shopping list and get it the next time.

However attractive the bargain, you should always ask yourself – was I planning to buy one of these? Would I ever have thought of buying one if I hadn't seen it on sale? Would I have missed it if I hadn't known about it? If the answer to each question is 'no' – well, you know what to do.

Imagine that on a visit to the sales you've spotted a brand new exercise bike, reduced all the way from £399 to £99. An irresistible bargain! However, to you, it's real value is exactly ZERO – because **you don't need it**.

Chris usually has little money available for 'frivolous' purchases, but for years he has kept a list of all the items he would like to buy if he had the money. Every time he thinks of a new item he'd like, he adds it to the list. The items range from a telephoto lens for his camera to a mandolin, a new pair of walking boots, a hand-made briefcase and various books and DVDs. When he sees an item on sale that is not on the list, however desirable it seems, he walks away – because he already knows that there are other things he wants more which should come first.

Retailers will play on your fear of missing out on a bargain and use all kinds of tricks to make an offer seem better than it is. It's astonishing how often, when you go away and do some research, you find that a similar item is available elsewhere at just as good a price or an even better one.

Our approach is challenging you to develop trust and faith that the item will still be available when you are ready to make the purchase. It's also challenging you to develop acceptance that you didn't **need** the thing after all, should it be sold out.

What do you do if you live in a rural area and are unlikely to return to town before the special offer ends? One way is to prepare for your trip by going through your larder, fridge and freezer thoroughly and making a note of anything you "could do with". You could then add it to your shopping list with a question mark. That way you give yourself permission to buy these items should they be on promotion. You could also give yourself an allowance to spend on anything, e.g. an introductory offer for a new product you would like to try out.

In the past you would have felt bad when you bought things on impulse. Now you make a conscious decision and feel good about your shopping experience.

CHAPTER 6

The light at the end of the tunnel

So far you may feel you've had to do a lot of work, but perhaps you're not sure just what you're going to get out of it. Trust us, a light is about to dawn!

But first, let's see – what do you do when you "lose the plot" and stop keeping your records and monitoring your cashflow? You do exactly what we suggested earlier, when you did your initial record keeping: when you forget to do it, try to catch up with yourself ONLY if you can easily reconstruct what's been happening. If not, start afresh.

It is also important to remember that if you keep forgetting to keep your books and therefore keep starting afresh, it does not mean that there is something wrong with you. Be patient with yourself. You are learning a completely new way of thinking about money.

You can start at any given moment in time. Do not wait until the beginning of a new week or month. Start *now*. Simply work out how much money you have for the rest of the month/period and allocate it in a cashflow plan. Then monitor your transactions against the plan as we suggested above.

Whether you have kept your books diligently over the planning period or whether you needed to start afresh doesn't really matter at the end of the month. We recommend that you do a final reckoning on the last day. It could look like this:

Sept		Plan	Received	Outstanding
INFLOWS				
I.1	Salary/Drawings (Aug.)	1,658	1,658.23	0
I.2	Child Support, Benefit (Aug.)	321	320.57	0
I.3	Gifts & Grants			
I.4	Misc.	34	33.99	0
	TOTAL	2,013	2,012.79	
OUTFLOWS		**Plan**	**Spent/Act**	**Remaining**
AP	Auto Payments	655	655.00	0
PP	Periodic Payments	134	134.00	0
SP	Special Purpose Savings	140	140.00	0
	Sub-Total	929	929.00	
	TOTAL AVAILABLE	1,084	1,083.79	
Day-to-Day				
1.	**Household**			
1.A	Groceries & Supplies	217	211.44	6
1.B	Children	180	179.50	0
1.C	Pets & Garden	36	34.20	2
1.D	Eat Out & Take Away Meals	48	48.00	0
2.	**Personal Care**			
2.A	Grooming/Make-up	52	48.99	3
2.B	Health Care	32	30.57	1
2.C	Body Work	45	45.00	0
3.	**Transport**			
3.A	Car	74	73.79	0
3.B	Public Transport & Taxis	15	12.45	3
4.	**Communication**			
4.A	Postage, Stationery, Consumables	44	44.31	0
4.B	Reference Books & Mags.	20	19.98	0
5.	**Leisure, Friends & Family**			
5.A	Hobbies	57	54.23	3
5.B	Entertainment/Fiction	112	105.25	7
5.C	Outings	117	117.00	0
5.D	Gifts etc.	35	33.60	1
	TOTAL	1,084	1,058.31	
Surplus		*0*	25.48	
Brought forward		*7*	*7.69*	
TOTAL SURPLUS		**7**	33.17	
Frivolity		*2*	1.98	0
Contingency		*2*	2.00	0
Debt Repayment		*3*	*3.00*	0
	TOTAL	*7*	6.98	
	OVERALL SURPLUS	**0**	**26**	

In our fictional example we made only the two adjustments we did earlier in the month. In real life it's much more likely that you will make quite a few changes during the course of the month. Remember that the purpose of the last column is not to tell you where you went "wrong" but to
  a) help you analyse what *actually* happened, and
  b) tell you how much money you have left to spend in each category, i.e. where you have room to manoeuvre.

In our example you are left with about £26. Now you check that against your transaction record, which looks like this:

		Cash	D2D account	Pay account
29.9.11	Balance	21.03	√4.29	√461.42
I.1	Salary/Drawings			1,658.23
30.9.11	Balance	21.03	4.29	2,119.65

Remember that for monitoring purposes we are only concerned with the balance in your "Day2Day" account and the actual cash in your pocket. If you add those two figures together you come to £25.32. If you round that to the nearest whole number you get £25, which is well within £2-3 of the £26 overall surplus of your cashflow plan.

The £2,119.65 in your "Pay" account is made up of the £320.57 Child support you received early in September, your salary of £1,658.23 and the £140.85 "cushion" you had in the account at the beginning of September when you allowed £134 for periodic payments, together with the buffer you added to your auto payments and the money that already was there at the start.

But, we hear you say, my account was overdrawn when I started. How does that work?

Let's say your transaction record looked like this when you started:

		Cash	D2D account	Pay account
31.8.11	Balance	4.68	0.00	-2,487.01
I.2 √	Child Support, Benefit (Aug.)			√+320.57
I.1 √	Salary/Drawings (Aug.)			√+1,658.23
1.9.11	Balance			-508.21

Even with the money you received in August the account remains overdrawn. If you withdraw the £1,084 you are planning to live on in September and all your regular payments go out won't you incur new unsecured debt? It may look like that on the surface, and initially the overdraft may seem to get bigger. But it does not, as you can see from our example below:

			Cash	D2D account	Pay account
31.8.11		Balance	4.68	0.00	-2,487.01
I.2 √		Child Support, Benefit (Aug.)			√+320.57
I.1 √		Salary/Drawings (Aug.)			√+1,658.23
1.9.11		Balance			-508.21
		From Pay a/c	xfer	√+1,084.00	√-1,084.00
AP √		Taxes (current)	DD		-331.60
AP √		Mortgage	DD		√-125.23
AP √		Health Insurance	DD		-35.64
AP √		Landline/ISP	DD		-18.58
AP √		Mobile/Cell	DD		-35.00
AP √		Pension	DD		√-74.90
AP √		Mortgage Arrears	DD		√-10.00
AP √		Back Taxes	DD		√-10.00
AP √		Credit Card	DD		√-10.00
Cont. √		Contingency	xfer	√-2.00	
DR √		Store Card (Debt Repay)	c01	-3.00	
		ATM	+50.00	√-50.00	
1.A √		Groceries	-14.13		
Friv. √		Coffee Shop ("Frivolity")	-1.98		
2.9.11		Balance	38.57	1,029.00	-2,243.16
SP √		Clothing & Accessories	xfer		√-50.00
SP √		Christmas	xfer		√-45.00
SP √		Summer Holiday	xfer		√-45.00
I.4 √		Refund (Mail Order Co.)			√+33.99
3.9.11		Balance	38.57	√1,029.00	√-2,349.17

However, there may be a slight dip whenever you make one of the periodic payments, such as the quarterly electricity bill, from the "Pay" account. For as long as you continue to include a buffer when you calculate the amount you need for the auto payments and round **up** the monthly amounts for your periodic payments to the nearest 1, you **will** see that your overdraft is gradually coming down, even when your bank adds interest.

When you allocate surplus/windfall funds you have a choice whether or not to include your overdraft in your total unsecured debt. For most people it depends on the amount available. If the amount is fairly small, many of our clients are happy to reduce the overdraft gradually through the measures described above. If the amount is fairly large, you might want to include the overdraft in your allocation.

Did you notice that we used the phrase "**when** you allocate surplus/windfall funds ..." in the last paragraph? That is because you **will** usually have a small surplus at the end of the month – if you are conscientious about keeping track of your money.

We suggest that you start drawing up the cashflow plan for the new month either immediately after you have finished the final reckoning on the last day, or the first day of the new month. You start with the data from your daily transaction record. Let's say it looks like this:

		Cash	D2D account	Pay account
29.9.11	Balance	21.03	√4.29	√461.42
l.1 √	Salary/Drawings			1,658.23
30.9.11	Balance	21.03	4.29	2,119.65

Remember we said earlier that the £2,119.65 in your "Pay account" is made up of the £320.57 Child support you received early in September, your salary of £1,658.23 and the £140.85 "cushion" you had in the account at the beginning of September when you allowed £134 for periodic payments together with the buffer you added to your auto payments and the money that was already there at the start.

The sum of the amounts in "Cash" and "D2D account", £25.32, is going to appear in your cashflow plan in the "brought forward" line. You always work with what you actually have left over, not what the cashflow says, because there is often a small discrepancy that would become bigger and bigger as you progress. So you start off like this:

Oct		Plan	Received	Outstanding
	INFLOWS			
I.1	Salary/Drawings (Sep.)	1,658	1,658.23	0
I.2	Child Support, Benefit (Sep.)	321	320.57	0
I.3	Gifts & Grants			
I.4	Misc			
	TOTAL	1,979	1,978.80	
	OUTFLOWS	Plan	Spent/Act	Remaining
AP	Auto Payments			
PP	Periodic Payments			
SP	Special Purpose Savings			
	Sub-Total			
	TOTAL AVAILABLE			
	Day-to-Day			
1.	**Household**			
1.A	Groceries & Supplies			
1.B	Children			
1.C	Pets & Garden			
1.D	Eat Out & Take Away Meals			
2.	**Personal Care**			
2.A	Grooming/Make-up			
2.B	Health Care			
2.C	Body Work			
3.	**Transport**			
3.A	Car			
3.B	Public Transport & Taxis			
4.	**Communication**			
4.A	Postage, Stationery, Consumables			
4.B	Reference Books & Mags.			
5.	**Leisure, Friends & Family**			
5.A	Hobbies			
5.B	Entertainment/Fiction			
5.C	Outings			
5.D	Gifts etc.			
	TOTAL			
	Surplus	*0*		
	Brought forward	*25*	*25.32*	
	TOTAL SURPLUS			
	Frivolity			
	Contingency			
	Debt Repayment			
	TOTAL			
	OVERALL SURPLUS			

All the other items are left blank because you basically start afresh every month. The actual figures and, especially, the variance analysis, are there to help you with your allocation. Remember that the analysis is there to answer the question: "Why was there a discrepancy?" The answers may be varied: something unforeseen happened, you forgot to include a heavier than usual expenditure in a category, or you simply under/overestimated expenditure.

As you did at the beginning of September, you start with your regular outflows, i.e. the auto and periodic payments, and the amounts you want to set aside.

Then you go through each discretionary category and reflect whether you are likely to spend the same amount in October or whether it's likely to be more or less. At the same time you need to think about what is likely to happen during the course of the month and how it impacts on money. For instance, British schools have a 1-week "half-term" holiday at the end of October. For our hypothetical family that means they expect to spend £60 less on extracurricular activities, which is included in their "Children" subcategory.

Do you remember that they decided to postpone an outing from September in order to live within their means? They are now planning to organise the outing during the half-term holiday, along with some other activities, so they increased their "Outings" subcategory to £150. They expect that all other expenditure will be roughly the same as in September.

Can you see in the plan below that there is now actually a surplus of £5? And without having to make an effort to restrict expenditure. This is what we mean when we say: "Live well within your means and your means expand." However, if you find that your planned outflows exceed your inflows, you need to repeat the exercise we gave you earlier, where you go through your categories one by one and see where you could reduce the planned expense.

The final plan for October looks like this:

Oct		Plan	Received	Outstanding
	INFLOWS			
I.1	Salary/Drawings (Sep.)	1,658	1,658.23	0
I.2	Child Support, Benefit (Sep.)	321	320.57	0
I.3	Gifts & Grants			
I.4	Misc			
	TOTAL	1,979	1,978.80	
	OUTFLOWS	**Plan**	**Spent/Act**	**Remaining**
AP	Auto Payments	655	655.00	0
PP	Periodic Payments	134	134.00	0
SP	Special Purpose Savings	140	140.00	0
	Sub-Total	929	929.00	
	TOTAL AVAILABLE	1,050	1,049.80	
	Day-to-Day			
1.	**Household**			
1.A	Groceries & Supplies	215		215
1.B	Children	120		120
1.C	Pets & Garden	35		35
1.D	Eat Out & Take Away Meals	48		48
2.	**Personal Care**			
2.A	Grooming/Make-up	50		50
2.B	Health Care	30		30
2.C	Body Work	45		45
3.	**Transport**			
3.A	Car	74		74
3.B	Public Transport & Taxis	12		12
4.	**Communication**			
4.A	Postage, Stationery, Consumables	44		44
4.B	Reference Books & Mags.	20		20
5	**Leisure, Friends & Family**			
5.A	Hobbies	55		55
5.B	Entertainment/Fiction	112		112
5.C	Outings	150		150
5.D	Gifts etc.	35		35
	TOTAL	**1,045**		
	Surplus	*5*		
	Brought forward	*25*	*25.32*	
	TOTAL SURPLUS	***30***	25.32	
	Frivolity	*10*		10
	Contingency	*10*		10
	Debt Repayment	*10*		10
	TOTAL	***30***		
	OVERALL SURPLUS	0		

Over time you will find that a small end-of-month surplus after you have allocated your available money becomes the norm. At last, you're on the home straight. Time to start thinking properly about the future.

CHAPTER 7

Achieving what really matters to YOU

What do you *really* want in life? Can money help you to achieve it, and if so, how?

We know people who appear to have hardly any money, yet are clearly living happy, fulfilled, lives. We also know people who make large salaries but feel that there is never enough, because they still can't afford the home they feel they ought to have, or the best schools for their children, or drive the kind of car that seems to befit their status. In this situation you could be on a six-figure or even seven-figure salary, yet never make it from one payday to the next.

If your priority is to live well and meet your **real** needs, the cashflow plan will help you identify these needs and how you can meet them appropriately within your current means. You might want to create your own "Hierarchy of Needs" to help you pinpoint what would be your ideal standard of living, not just in terms of money but how you want to live your life.

You already started doing that when you decided the order of your main spending categories. When you create this personal "Hierarchy of Needs" you need to include the items from your Auto Payments and Set Aside lists. As a result your categories might be grouped slightly differently. Now you go through each group and decide for yourself what would be the most basic, or survival, level, what would be your ideal, or luxury, level and what would be the level in between. For instance you might create a scale of 1-5, where level 1 is "survival" and level 5 "luxury".

This is how some categories might look like for a single person:

FOOD/WATER

Level 1 – drinkable water; enough food to survive
Level 2 – choice of beverages; nourishing, tasty food with variety; occasional take-away meals
Level 3 – some organic and/or locally produced food; convenience food; occasional meals at cheap chain restaurants or local cafés
Level 4 – mainly organic and/or locally produced food; eat out more often at affordable restaurants
Level 5 – mainly organic and/or locally produced food; someone cooking lunch for me most days; eat out whenever and wherever I choose, including top restaurants

TRANSPORT

Level 1 – enough money for public transport; lifts from friends
Level 2 – enough money for public transport (incl. cheap rail, coach and air travel); occasional taxi; lifts from friends; savings fund for car purchase

Level 3 – functional, reliable second-hand car; money for fuel, insurance, road tax, car maintenance, repairs, parking; savings fund for car replacement; enough money to take public transport (incl. rail, coach and air travel) and taxis, when appropriate

Level 4 – new reliable car; money for fuel, insurance, road tax, car maintenance, repairs, parking; savings fund for car replacement; enough money to take public transport (incl. rail, coach and air travel, business class on longer flights) and taxis, when desired

Level 5 – new car of my dreams, money for fuel, insurance, road tax, car maintenance, repairs, parking; enough money in car replacement fund to change it at least every other year, use of public transport (1st class), taxis, or hired cars (with or without chauffeur) when desired

INCOME GENERATION

Level 1 – ensure I receive all social security benefits I am entitled to, ensure that payments towards state retirement pension scheme continue

Level 2 – work part-time for an employer

Level 3 – work part-time for an employer + work part-time from home on a self-employed basis, doing the thing I really love. My business generates sufficient income for me to live on a mixture of drawings and salary. Pay National Insurance and all other required social security contributions

Level 4 – work full-time on a self-employed basis, doing the thing I really love. Rent business premises in a decent building/location. Have money for a part-time assistant. Pay National Insurance and all other required social security contributions + income replacement insurance premiums. My business generates sufficient income for me to live prosperously within a realistic cashflow plan

Level 5 – I have largely retired from my business, the business is located in a building I own; I have a PA; my investments and other sources generate sufficient income for me to live prosperously within my ideal cashflow plan; I only "work" as much or as little as I want to.

DEBT REPAYMENT

Level 1 – nothing can be repaid
Level 2 – more than zero: £1(+) per month
Level 3 – more than £25 per month to each creditor
Level 4 – more than £200 to each creditor
Level 5 – no debt at all to repay – ever again!

Other groupings to consider are:
Housing
Children
Healthcare
Personal care
Clothing/shoes/accessories
Communication: telephone/internet/postage

Entertainment/social
Rest/relaxation/adventure
Savings
Tithing
Taxes

Living your dream

Now we can start to enjoy ourselves – on paper, at least. Did you notice that our fictional person mentions an "ideal cashflow plan" under Income Generation (Level 5)? That's the next exercise you might want to do. Go through your Hierarchy of Needs and try to estimate how much you would need to spend in each of your categories if you wanted to live at the luxury level (this would be your net income, i.e. after tax, so you may need to add on the percentage of income tax you'd be likely to pay). This will give you the income you would need to have to live the way you really want to.

The amount you wind up with might appear to be totally out of reach. But remember that the purpose of the exercise is to help you to identify your real needs and desires. Like the list of 100 ways in which more money could come into your life, it is helpful to review your Hierarchy of Needs once in a while. You'll find that it changes over time. For some it may need to expand even more, while for others it becomes more "realistic".

We have noticed an interesting phenomenon. The things we want to do or have when we've reached luxury level seem to come into our lives, sometimes in quite unexpected ways. Susie, for instance, has a long-term health condition which is making her increasingly disabled. She had written "someone cooking lunch for me" in her Hierarchy of Needs. It seemed that in "absolutely no time" she was given this option. Moreover, a benevolent fund offered a monthly grant to pay for the meals.

Back to the waterfall. Do you remember that we said that you could not see where the water (money) was coming from, only that it keeps coming – and not only that, but that it keeps coming in abundance. This happens if we try to stop working out in our heads where money might come from and remain open to possibilities we could not even conceive of. This is what happened to Lisa and Daniel (Chapter 3) when out of the blue they were offered a way of reducing their major debt.

Besides remaining open to new and unexpected sources of money, it seems that a commitment to living within one's means is a prerequisite to these things happening. As you've learned, this depends on scrupulous record-keeping and cashflow monitoring.

This might be more difficult to maintain then you thought. You may find that you experience a lot of resistance. You may also find that many emotional issues are brought to the surface, not all of which you may have been aware of. In extreme cases you might even need to seek professional help.

This is not surprising. After all, most people seem to associate money with safety. It has been said that we try to stay safe by predicting the future. Apparently we do that by looking in the past and assuming that the future will be similar, and by continuing to do what we've done in the past. It follows that, since safety is vital to our very survival, we can expect to feel some strong emotions when we're challenged to change the way we deal with money.

It's also a matter of control. As long as we think we know where our money is coming from, we have a sense of being in control. Now we are challenging you to have faith, and trust that more money will come into your life from **somewhere**, even though you have no idea where.

Dreams, goals and visions

Now let's focus on the future, and think where you would like to be say in six months, a year, two years, five years – not only in terms of money, but your external (material/physical) and internal (personal) environment.

Your external environment includes where you would like to live and in what kind of home, how you would like to dress, how you would like to get around etc. The internal environment includes how you feel about yourself, how you relate to other people, what kind of people are in your life and so on.

What are your dreams and goals? We call this having a vision. Each person's vision is unique, and yet in each of us our vision serves the same purpose. Based on the idea that we live in an orderly universe, each person's vision fits in somehow with everybody else's. It's when we let our fears, anxieties, and self-doubts get in the way that we come into conflict with others, creating all sorts of problems for ourselves and the people around us.

If we ignore or deny our vision we are likely to have a sense of aimlessness, irritability and resentment, increased fear and anxiety and decreased self-esteem, along with a sense of failure. Yet, many of us keep ourselves so busy doing what we "have to do" that we don't get around to asking ourselves what we **really** want to do, who we want to be, what we want to have. Sometimes we don't know how to differentiate between what we really want and what we think we should want.

So, how do you find your own vision? If you created a personal Hierarchy of Needs you have already taken a significant step towards it. Whatever you have written down in your "luxury" level will give you a good clue. At this point you may actually want to review your Hierarchy of Needs. Is what you wrote then what you still want now?

What do you **really** want to be, have, or do in the following areas of your life in ...... months/years time, in the areas of

- Housing
- Money
- Work

- Relationships
- Family
- Health
- Spiritual
- Leisure
- Anything else?

Then write a little essay. You could give it a title like *"A vision for my life, summer 2020"*.

It's important to make short positive statements in the present tense, as if it is already reality. Avoid sayings things like "I can...", "I am able to ...", I have achieved ...". Instead use "I ... (do/have)".

Here is one example: "I am debt-free. I have a secure and plentiful income. My earned income derives from work which I thoroughly enjoy and makes a difference. I am valued, respected and supported by my colleagues and clients/customers. I have a passive income from sound investments. I live in a ... house in ... My home is furnished with good quality furniture. It is adorned with original art. I pay someone to do all my housework. I drive a ... I wear designer clothes and footwear. I use luxury cosmetic products and toiletries. I use an upmarket hairdresser/barber. I have plenty of time and money to pamper myself with massages, beauty therapies and spa breaks. I go on exotic holidays. I travel in comfort, first class. I have all necessary insurance in place. There is enough money in my contingency fund to cover at least ... months living costs and any unforeseen expenses. I have adequate pension arrangements to maintain a prosperous lifestyle in retirement."

An alternative way is to approach it like a timeline, or taking notes for an autobiography. You write about things you would like to happen in the future as if they happened in the past and/or are ongoing. Using this approach the above vision might look like this:

- ✔ I have been free of unsecured debt since .... 20...
- ✔ In the spring/summer/autumn/winter of 20... I bought a house in ...
- ✔ I paid off my mortgage .... 20... and own my home outright.
- ✔ My home is furnished with good quality furniture.
- ✔ In the spring/summer/autumn/winter of 20... I bought my first piece of original art by ....
- ✔ I have been employing someone to do all my housework since spring/summer/ autumn/winter 20...
- ✔ I started work at .... in the spring/summer/autumn/winter of 20... My work makes a difference. I thoroughly enjoy every minute of it.
- ✔ I am valued, respected and supported by my colleagues and clients/customers.
- ✔ In the spring/summer/autumn/winter 20... I bought a brand new .... I have replaced this car with a new one every other year since.
- ✔ In the spring/summer/autumn/winter 20... I bought my first tailor-made suit/hand-made pair of shoes. They are professionally looked after and replaced as and when necessary.

✔ Since spring/summer/autumn/winter 20... I buy ... cosmetic products and ... toiletries

You get the drift!

Of course, not everyone would want to buy a new car every other year, even if they could – an increasing number of us would opt for a reliable eco-friendly model and keep it throughout its serviceable life – and some millionaires prefer to do their own housework! The point is that these are *your* choices.

Some of our clients then go on to formulate an "ideal cashflow plan" which reflects how much money they might need to finance this vision. Tom did, and within months applied for a job which offered him the necessary salary "to the penny". However, others find this exercise unhelpful. It makes them feel frustrated and discouraged; that they will never be able to achieve their vision. You have to decide for yourself which is right for you.

How is a "vision" different from setting goals or objectives? We believe it changes the way you view the outcomes and and go about achieving them. When you set yourself goals and objectives and then start wheeling, dealing and manipulating to realise the outcomes, you put yourself in the driving seat. That will create stress and pressure, and give you a sense of failure when those goals/objectives are not achieved. If you believe in a god and practise prayer your prayer might be: "Let me achieve ...."

With a vision, you let go of specific outcomes. Instead you open yourself out to the abundance and benevolence of the universe by adopting the "act as if" approach. This is a useful tool to help overcome self-limiting beliefs and doubts. You act as if your desired outcome has been achieved already, and your mind follows – you actually start believing that it is possible, and the universe responds. Here your prayer would probably be in the form of a question, such as: "How can I 'act as if'?" or: "What needs to happen about this vision?"

In our experience the universe, or God, if you prefer, typically responds in two ways. An idea suddenly pops into your head; often something that hasn't even remotely occurred to you before. The other response might be that something totally unexpected happens which then makes your next step obvious. Then you need to follow through with the action.

This vision approach also helps you to discern whether what you want is in alignment with the universe, or God's will, if you like. By taking things slowly, one step at a time, your desire may get stronger and things seem to just fall into place. Alternatively, as time passes, your desire diminishes or disappears altogether, or whichever way you turn you seem to run into brick walls. This doesn't necessarily mean your desire is out of alignment with the universe. Perhaps the timing isn't right, or it needs a little bit of tweaking.

When Stephen lived in a social housing studio apartment in the inner city, he wrote in his vision that he had moved to a larger home in the suburbs. His first action towards realising that vision was to create a separate savings account to save up for the move. He then made enquiries with a number of social landlords. He also made some low-cost changes to his apartment, which reflected the vision of his ideal home. He took all these actions as time and money allowed but with a steady purpose. Then an unexpected solution presented itself. The whole process, from writing down his vision to actually moving into his "dream home", took about 2 years. He is very happy there and has no desire to move.

This brings us neatly to creating a savings strategy. We recommend that you have at least two savings accounts. Let's go back to our family. Do you remember that they set aside a certain sum every month towards expected events? Then they opened two savings accounts, one for their "Clothing Fund" and one for "Special Purpose Savings". When you do that, you need to think about how easy, or difficult, you want to make it for yourself to access those funds.

Stephanie opened an e-savings account, linked to her current account. After only a few months she found that she still struggled to live within her means and continuously "dipped" into the savings to make up the resulting shortfall. In the end she decided to open a savings account with a different bank and set up a standing order to automatically transfer the money she wanted to set aside. That way she made it more difficult for herself to access these funds. She also declined the options of an ATM card and online and telephone banking facilities, so she had to make a special trip to withdraw any funds.

Accordingly, the list for "Special Purpose Savings" in our example, linked to the cashflow plan, looked like this:

What	Amount	Where to
Clothing & Accessories	50	Clothing Fund
Christmas	45	Special Purpose Savings
Summer Holiday	45	Special Purpose Savings
TOTAL	**140**	

You keep track of the movements in your savings account in a similar way to your daily transaction record and the way you tracked your debts. For instance, our family decided to open two savings accounts for their "Special Purpose Savings"; one for Christmas and their summer holiday, and a separate one for a "Clothing Fund". They also decided to use a simple cashbook for their "Clothing Fund". It could look like this:

		In	Out	Bal.
2.9.11	From "Pay A/c"	50.00		50.00
3.10.11	From "Pay A/c"	50.00		100.00
24.10.11	To "D2D A/c" (Jumper)		29.95	70.05
1.11.11	From "Pay A/c"	50.00		120.05
2.12.11	From "Pay A/c"	50.00		170.05
14.12.11	To "D2D A/c" (Chrismas outfits)		132.47	37.58
4.1.12	From "Pay A/c"	50.00		87.58
8.1.12	To "D2D A/c" (Shoes)		54.99	32.59
1.2.12	From "Pay A/c"	50.00		82.59
3.3.12	From "Pay A/c"	50.00		132.59
2.4.12	From "Pay A/c"	50.00		182.59

Did you notice that they always transferred the exact amount into their "D2D account"? Doing it that way helps to keep these transactions separate from their normal spending. It is also helpful to leave the first column in the daily transaction record blank, or use a symbol like an asterisk, to make it clear that the transactions relating to the purchase of items funded from savings are outside the normal cashflow plan.

The transaction record for their Special Purpose Savings" looks slightly different:

	Christmas	Summer Holiday	TOTAL
2.9.11	45.00	45.00	90.00
Balance	45.00	45.00	90.00
3.10.11	45.00	45.00	90.00
Balance	90.00	90.00	180.00
1.11.11	45.00	45.00	90.00
Balance	135.00	135.00	270.00
2.12.11	45.00	45.00	90.00
Balance	180.00	180.00	360.00
5.12.11	-150.00		-150.00
Balance	30.00	180.00	210.00
17.12.11	-30.00		-30.00
Balance	0.00	180.00	180.00

When you draw up your cashflow plan for any month in which you plan to draw on your savings, we recommend that you add another line to the inflows; e.g. "I.5 from Savings". You then have the choice of either adding another outflow category such as "Holiday", or incorporating the extra funds available into the existing categories.

Lastly you need a record for your contingency fund. It could look similar to the "Clothing Fund". Remember that your contingency fund is for unexpected expenditure and/or emergencies. Therefore you need to have a savings account you can draw on quickly, such as internet savings. But make sure to keep it separate from your other savings. That will help you keep it separate in your mind and help you resist the temptation to draw on it when things get "a bit tight".

You might think that the amounts you put in are so small that it's hardly worth bothering, but if you consistently apply the 3-way split to any surplus funds and/ or windfalls you'll be surprised how quickly it builds up. You might then even find yourself reluctant to draw on it when you need to.

This was the case when Liz and Joe's roof started to leak and they had to ransack their contingency fund. Initially they were quite despondent about the fact that they had to start building up the contingency fund again, but Sanni pointed out that thanks to the fund they did not need to incur any debt. Remember that this is exactly the purpose of the contingency fund: to stand between you and debt.

Discovering your potential, and fulfilling it

Once you start taking actions towards achieving your goals, you may discover that your vision is changing or expanding. In this way you are being challenged to fulfil your true potential – your mission, if you like. We like to call it your primary purpose, the thing you have been put on this planet to do.

We are convinced that everyone has come into this world with a unique set of gifts and talents that equip them for their specific purpose. All the experiences they have had, all the challenges they have faced, the problems they have overcome, are designed to develop their skills to fulfil that primary purpose, or, as some people call it, their primary intent.

Look back over your life and the choices you have made. They will give you a pointer towards what your primary purpose might be. Other pointers come from your hierarchy of needs and the vision you have defined, as well as the list of 100 ways of bringing more money into your life. (By the way, this might be a good time to repeat the exercise.)

At this point you might want to write a "mission statement" for your life as some big organisations do. This statement should be one or two sentences, up to 30 to 40 words. It may take a few weeks before something that you *know* is right emerges.

Here is Sanni's statement: "My mission is to be a shining example of how the effects of a traumatic childhood can be transformed into assets for a happy, fulfilled and prosperous life."

The mission statement will give the clearest indication what your primary intent is. Since every person has been put on this planet to *do* something, the primary purpose must be a verb; just one. This could be something like: to create, to heal, to teach, to entertain, to learn, to compete, to listen etc.

When you look back over your life you may well discover that most of the things you have done in your life, both professionally and personally, have an element of your primary intent. Erika discovered that her primary purpose is to listen – she is a psychiatric nurse. Sometimes the link is not quite so obvious. For instance Richard, a management consultant, has identified "to create" as his primary intent. This might seem tricky in his profession, but he says that he will only accept an assignment if he can see a creative element within it.

When you live your vision and fulfil your primary purpose, you align your will with the order and rhythm of the universe. Then your life becomes like a dance. You live with joy, love and self-worth. You will achieve a level of emotional balance, prosperity and inner peace you never thought possible.

The American preacher Howard Thurman once said: *"Don't just ask what the world needs. Ask what makes you come alive and then go and do it, because what the world needs is people who have come alive."*

Eventually, you will realise that living your vision is the best gift you can give to others. Your personal contentment and example will inspire them to do the same. Thus more and more people dare to do what makes their heart sing; i.e. live according their primary intent, and somehow that it "all kind of fits together".

Keeping up with the bookkeeping may seem like a lot of hard work and a lot of books to keep. But it is this element that keeps your feet firmly on the ground and enables you to live well "in the real world".

Think of life as a journey into the unknown. Wherever and however you travel, even if it's only across your living room, you are bound to look out for signposts and landmarks to determine your position in relation to your surroundings and check your progress. Bookkeeping fulfils that function.

It may well be difficult in the early stages, partly because you're learning a completely new way of handling money and partly because there may be some emotional fallout. The strength of this must not be underestimated – it is likely to discourage you from persevering with this programme. But it is vastly different from juggling your debt, trying to work out in your head how to pay your bills, which credit card to use in the shops, how to make the minimum repayments or pay the mortgage. Instead you'll find that you start to juggle your own money in the various saving funds, as well the day-to-day cashflow plan. Most of our clients tell us that, once they get the hang of this, they really enjoy doing it.

Let's look at which records you should have:

1. Your daily record of transactions. This is most vital because it gives you all the data you need to work with. Even if you fall by the wayside and fail to keep up with anything else, maintaining this record enables you to either reconstruct or start again, **based on fact**.
2. The cashflow plan for the coming period. It is the heart of your money management, where all the information from the other records are computed.

3. The records of your
    a. Automated payments
    b. Monthly amounts for your Periodic payments
    c. Monthly "Set aside" savings amounts
4. The list of all debtors with a record of repayments and debt still to pay.
5. A record of your contingency fund
6. A record of any other savings funds

We suggest that you keep all the books in an easily accessible place. That should encourage you to maintain them conscientiously. If you use spreadsheets you could use different worksheets in the same document and link them.

You might want to use a software package. If you think back on the analogy of being on a journey, software acts like a satellite navigation system. It keeps everything in one place and updates all the relevant books with just one or two entries. Our own software is designed to complement our approach. It's available at
http://www.holisticmoneymanager.com/software/

As you progress with this programme your income will gradually increase, your debts will be paid off and you'll have more money available for day-to-day spending. Before long you may find that more and more of the "luxury" items in your Hierarchy of Needs appear in your day-to-day cashflow plan, as well as those which at the start were considered "Frivolity".

What do you do with any surplus once your unsecured debts are all paid off? Any financial adviser will recommend that for as long as you have **any** debt whatsoever, such as a mortgage or a finance deal on a car, you should work towards paying that off early. This is simply because usually the interest you pay is higher than any interest you earn on savings. Therefore we suggest you continue to either overpay your mortgage payments with the third from your surplus or windfalls which you allocate towards "debt repayments", or save it to make a lump sum payment.

What do you do if you have reached that wonderful position where you have no debt whatsoever? We suggest that you continue to divide any surplus funds by 3 and allocate the 1/3 that was assigned to "debt repayment" to long-term savings, to build up capital or an additional pension fund. Consult a financial adviser who can help you decide what is best for your individual situation.

You may think that the amounts you have available for long-term savings will be too small to be worth troubling a financial adviser. In that case we suggest that you open another savings account and build up a lump sum.

What do you do about charitable giving or tithing? We said earlier that some of our clients feel they have to give away 10% of their income to their church or charity. This may lead to distress if they then struggle to meet their own needs. We advocate amending the formula for your surplus/windfall funds as follows: 10% to charity/church and then 30% (one third) each to "frivolity", "contingency" and "debt repayment".

There is a second option, which we call the "Prosperity Formula". Here you use one half, or 50%, for your day-to-day spending. The remaining 50% gets divided into five equal parts, i.e. 10% to charity and 10% each into various savings funds for specific purposes, e.g. replacement funds for car(s), furniture, home appliances etc., and/or to build up an investment/pension lump sum.

Some of our clients apply this formula to all their income, others to surplus and windfall funds, yet others only to windfall income. We have shown you how to choose the right option. Your final decision whether to continue with the 3-way split or the "Prosperity Formula", or a combination of the two, will depend on your specific circumstances. Remember, too, that you can always change your approach.

Let's go back to the waterfall again. Most of the water flows straight out of the main basin into the stream. This is your day-to-day spending. There are rock pools around the main basin where water is swirling in and out. The smaller ones near the main basin constantly fill up and empty. These are your various special purpose saving funds. The larger rock pools at the back need longer to fill up but don't seem to fully empty out either, just overflow at times. These are your contingency fund and/or long-term savings. And there is mist in the air which is nourishing lichen growing on the rocks all around the waterfall. This is the abundance you give away to charity.

Also remember that from where you stand it is impossible to see where the water is coming from. It's not important for you to know. What is important is the fact that it keeps coming.

Living prosperously

Sanni likes to think of life as a journey into the unknown. On any journey you need to know what you need along the way, where you are going, why you are going there, and where you are at each moment along the way. Never more so than with the journey of life.

Even on the shortest of journeys (let's say you are just popping out to see a neighbour) you will think about whether you need to change your shoes before you set off, take your key to get back in the house, put on a coat etc. Obviously you need to know where you're going. You also you need to think about what you're going to do when you get there – e.g. will you be sitting down with your neighbour, or just talk on the doorstep? Thirdly you need to know why you are going, for instance to have a chat or to ask them to take in a parcel for you. Lastly, while you are on your way you constantly use your eyes and other senses to inform you where you are and how much further you have to go.

On our journey through life we need to be clear about our real needs. This is the first element of prosperity. Both our vision and your cashflow planning give us this clarity. The second element is a clear vision of our life. As with the visit to our neighbour, we need to know where we want to go and what we want to do when you get there. The third element is clarity about our mission and purpose in life – i.e. knowing why we are going. The fourth element is the clarity about our finances – about knowing how much money you have, where and for what – which tells us where we are and how much further we have to go.

This book concentrates heavily on the fourth element, the bookkeeping. We learn how to orientate ourselves in our physical environment when we are babies and do it without being consciously aware that we are doing it. Now you have to learn consciously how to orientate yourself financially.

Once all four elements are in place you have everything you need to live prosperously. No matter what happens in your life as long as you maintain clarity about them, you will have choices and be able to adapt your money management to your circumstances. This programme will have given you this. Good luck!

www.ingramcontent.com/pod-product-compliance
Lightning Source LLC
Chambersburg PA
CBHW060636210326
41520CB00010B/1624